TONI AND MARKUS

TONI AND MARKUS

*From Village Life
to Urban Stress*

WALTER ROTH

Toni and Markus: From Village Life to Urban Stress
Copyright 2014 by Walter Roth

Published by Walter Roth, Chicago, IL
walterjroth@gmail.com
First edition, 2014

ISBN-13: 978-0692225882
ISBN-10: 0692225889

*In memory of
my mother Selma, my father Markus,
my stepmother Toni, and my sister Irene*

TABLE OF CONTENTS

PREFACE

This book confronts the challenges my father Markus, stepmother Toni, and their family faced in creating a new life in the city of Chicago, after they were forced, in 1938, to leave behind their village life in Roth, Germany in the wake of Nazi persecution. The book first sets forth a dialogue between Toni and me that gives a more detailed look at Toni and Markus' life in Germany. We hear, in her own words, about her early life and her marriage to Markus—how Toni and Markus united the Roth and Stern families.

The book continues with Toni and Markus' life in Chicago and the problems they faced in this new environment. Some of the material involves sensitive and personal problems, which I hope I have written about with the depth of feeling called for. We talk about Markus and his struggles to make a living in the Chicago stockyards. We hear from Toni about her attempts to care for her family. We discuss the painful problems of my sister Irene, and Markus' problems as well. In my discussions with Toni I believe we gain an understanding and greater insight into these problems. We also learn about some of the joy Toni was able to transmit in her almost 100 years of life.

INTRODUCTION

In writing this book, I aim to pay tribute to my father Markus Roth, my stepmother Toni Stern Roth, my sister Irene, and my mother Selma. Selma died in 1934 when I was five years old. Two years after her death my father married Toni, who happened to be a cousin of Selma's. Toni became the family matriarch, and I grew up calling her mother. In June 1938 my family, including Toni, Markus, my older brother Herb, my older sister Irene, and myself, fled from the village of Roth, Germany. [The family name Roth and the village name Roth are only coincidentally the same.] Toni was pregnant at the time of our escape. Six months after we arrived in America, where we settled in Chicago, Toni gave birth to my younger sister Helen.

While the story of Jews who survived the Holocaust in hiding in Europe is well known, less has been written about those Jews who left Europe as refugees from the Nazi regime in the years leading up to World War II. Those who managed to escape were often poverty-stricken and forced to live in a strange world of unfamiliar languages and culture.

My family's story is of that type of immigrant. Growing up in a poor immigrant household in Chicago was not easy, but that childhood experience shaped my life and values. Even within our family there were differences in what we experienced. Herb and Irene spent most of their childhoods in Germany, I spent only my first nine years there, and of course Helen was born in the United States. Although we shared family and some experiences, there were differences in childhood and perceptions. I saw my father and Toni—my parents—go from having a simple Jewish life in a tiny historic village in central Germany, with a small but strong circle of family and community, to living a complex immigrant existence in a new country. Though they were educated individuals, they seemed to become lost and broken by the many new challenges stacked against them when they were transplanted. Helen knew only of life with my parents in Chicago. She had different impressions of events than the rest of us because she spent so much more time living with our parents during their early years in Chicago.

Though we never spoke about my parents' difficulties while I was growing up, it became of much more interest to me as I grew older and came to terms with my own challenges. The impact of the Shoah undoubtedly contributed to the early deaths of my father and my sister Irene.

In my 2013 book, *Departure and Return: Trips to and Memories From Roth, Germany*, I recounted some of the history and life in the village of Roth and its surroundings. Now I would like to recount in more depth the lives of Toni and Markus, and of Irene, in Roth and in Chicago. This account is based on several recorded conversations with my mother Toni, my sister Helen, and other family members, some of which were moderated by my daughter, Miriam. The interviews include a long session with Toni on November 6, 1988, when she was 90 years old. At that time she was living at the Selfhelp Home, a retirement home established in Chicago in the 1930s by German Jewish immigrants, first in Hyde Park and later in Uptown. Additional conversations arose out of the visits that my wife Chaya, our children Ari, Judy and Miriam, and our seven grandchildren have made to Roth, Germany to explore the history of our family in the village. In this book, I have combined and consolidated several of these family conversations, which span a 20 year period, in order to tell the story. I have put these conversations together to create a picture of my stepmother Toni and the challenges she faced alongside my father. This book is not a verbatim transcript of interviews, but rather an edited and clarified text comprised of conversations, combined with my impressions and memories.

I would like to thank Chaya, my children, and my sister Helen for reading and commenting on this text; my brother-in-law Lowell Dittmer for translations; my brother Herb for permission to use material from his publication *The Stern Family in Roth*; my niece Debbie Roth-Howe for sharing her work on family recipes; Rabbi Elliot B. Gertel for permission to include his eulogy of Toni; and my assistant Susan Rosenberg for her work with me on this text.

LIFE IN ROTH, GERMANY

Toni's Childhood and Youth

Wally: I am sitting down with mother, well actually stepmother…

Toni: Yes, I married your father in 1936.

Wally: We are going to talk about your life and the experience of growing up in Germany and moving to the United States. Mother is currently 90 years old and living at the Selfhelp Home. I really want to make sure we talk about my siblings Herb, Helen, and Irene, as well as Dad. And Mother, please be as truthful as possible. Tell me about your life growing up.

Toni: I suppose we should start with my mother, Berta. She was a tough cookie… the "boss". I really admired her so much—to the point I think someone once accused me of worshiping her. I suppose I looked to her so much for strength, especially after I left Germany for Chicago—it might have easily looked as if I worshiped her. She was the oldest of 10 children, so no wonder she was the boss. She came from Borken [a nearby village]. You and I are related on your mother [Selma's] side. My grandfather [Bonfang

Stern, Toni's paternal grandfather] was Selma's great uncle.

My other grandfather [Feist Rosenbusch, Toni's maternal grandfather] had a rough life near the end. Under German Jewish tradition, when the oldest son got married he effectively became the owner of the family's house. The oldest son's parents could continue to live there and were guaranteed a room downstairs, but that's it. And so, in this particular situation, there was somewhat of a scandal because Berta's oldest brother didn't honor that rule.

Wally: Oh, I remember, I did hear this story.

Toni: And the oldest brother was very mean to his father—whether the brother evicted his father or didn't give him the room he was entitled to, I'm not sure. Mother always held that against her brother. And I felt the same, even once we moved to Chicago. Berta's brother got out of Germany and came to Chicago, and lived on 52nd and Blackstone near us in Hyde Park. It always pained me to see him, especially knowing that not only had he disrespected his father but also that the others didn't make it out of Germany.

Wally: Oh, that's just terrible. What did Berta do when the oldest brother took over the house?

Toni: Well I think she was gone and married by that point. My older brother Louis was born in 1894. So I think my parents were married in 1893. And my next brother, Hugo, was born in 1896.

Wally: And where did Berta meet your father?

Toni: In Borken. My uncle married a woman named Hilda Bachenheimer and through Hilda, my father met my mother, Berta. Hilda was from a nearby village called Fronhausen. Another Bachenheimer married my mother's sister Ida Rosenbush.

Wally: So, when they got married, your mother moved to Roth.

Toni: Yes, and I was born in 1898, on the 21st of July, in Roth.

Wally: Do you remember when you were born?

Toni: I think not (laughs).

Wally: Well, what's the first thing that you can remember when you were a young person?

Toni: Oh, I don't know.

Wally: Where did you live when you were young?

Toni: In an apartment that my parents rented. It was in the Nathans' house. We lived upstairs and they lived downstairs. The people didn't get real nervous then sharing a house with two families. It was a good life.

Wally: Do you think it was an easier life then?

Toni: Well, you missed some things. After all, you didn't hear and see much from the world.

Wally: You didn't have any television?

Toni: (Laughs) No, only the radio. Television came later.

Wally: No telephone?

Toni: Not when I was growing up, but your father had a telephone in the house when we were married. People didn't have a phone. Or very few did.

Wally: Did you have a washroom in the house?

Toni: Outside. It was wonderful (laughs).

Wally: And what about hot water?

Toni: It was in the kitchen, in the kitchen stove. There was a bar on the side of the stove. It was a steel rod on which we could hang the water pail to heat. And then we kept the stove burning most of the time. They had something that kept it burning. Grits we called it [little pieces of coal or wood] to make the water hot. And it stayed hot.

Wally: So, where and when did you take a bath?

Toni: Not every day. It wasn't that easy. But people didn't get so dirty then either.

Wally: Oh, so they didn't smell as much then as they do today?

Toni: I don't know. It depends on how much people work today.

Wally: Did you have a bathtub?

Toni: Some people had one later. We didn't have one.

Wally: So how did you take a bath?

Toni: We had a round basin in the kitchen. There was just one for all of us. Everything was a little… little different.

Wally: So you had one stove in the kitchen. Was there another stove in the house?

Toni: Yes, in the dining room.

Wally: Was the dining room in the main part of the house?

Toni: Yes, it was also the living room. Also, some people in the town even had a stove in the bedroom. I think one person I knew who had a stove in the bedroom was my aunt Hilda—she had a bedroom stove.

Wally: But you didn't have one.

Toni: No, but it was all right; the bedroom was right over the living room.

Wally: But I would imagine at night in the winter it got pretty cold?

Toni: Yes, yes. There was not the convenience we have now with central heat.

Wally: So how long did Berta and your father rent this apartment? Wasn't it about the late 1920's that your parents started building their own house?

Toni: They started building it in 1929.

Wally: Did you live anyplace else before that time?

Toni: We lived by the neighbors, the Ruth's.

Wally: You know, the Ruth's daughter says she was my first kiss. I'm periodically still in touch with her. I actually didn't remember, but when I went back she was insistent that I was her boyfriend before we left Germany.

Toni: I doubt it.

Wally: Hah. Well where else did you live?

Toni: We moved to the Seligmann's house, which was not very comfortable. From there we moved into our own house that we built. When we were building it, someone not from Roth came to my parents' house and told them they shouldn't build a house because they were "going to be thrown out of Germany anyway."

Wally: How much anti-Semitism was there in the town at that time?

Toni: It was early then; that was one of the few comments I remember. It was much different later when you were growing up in Roth.

Wally: I seem to remember in Roth, itself, that there were two guys who led it all. The teacher was one; however he was a replacement teacher.

Toni: Yes, the old guy who was the original teacher was not anti-Semitic, but the new teacher they had right before we left was a Nazi. The old teacher was arrested. But Roth had no priest. That was the big thing. So they didn't have anybody preaching Nazism. Additionally, I recall you were a couple times accosted by kids, but they were not from Roth—it was nothing like in the big cities.

Wally: Back to your childhood; what work did your father do?

Toni: He sold dry goods. There were two brothers; my father and his older brother. They owned the business together.

Wally: And they had a wagon?

Toni: Not always, eventually they did.

Wally: And a horse?

Toni: Not in the beginning. That's later on.

Wally: Where did you buy food and supplies?

Toni: When I was growing up my family went to a corner shop in town to get nearly all our foodstuffs. It was a great shop, around for years. It was not a big store, but I never saw such a clean, organized place. It was there when you children were growing up too. If you were to ask your brother, he would know it. Only he would probably remember it only for their candies. He ate so many sweets as a boy.

Wally: That was right near where your parents' house was before you moved in with my father and us. And was still there last time I was there in the 1980s.

Toni: The owner, old man Sauer, took care of the store and his children helped him; and he was a smart one too. He went to America once he had enough money; it was probably around when he was first married. I don't know how he made it there, but more surprising was that he came back to Germany. He had then four children around. He was successful in America and with that money he built his house and store. He had land too.

Wally: Wasn't there another store in Roth where they sold candy for the kids?

Toni: Yes. Your brother frequented that one too! It was owned by a different family, but equally frequented by your brother for candy. It was right next to the synagogue in Roth.

Wally: Speaking of synagogue, when did you go to synagogue; you as a girl?

Toni: In Roth?

Wally: Yes.

Toni: Friday night and Saturday. Or when something special was happening like Purim or Passover.

Wally: Holidays?

Toni: Holidays. Yes, we went.

Wally: Why wasn't the synagogue burned down [on Kristallnacht in 1938, which occurred in the area of Roth one day earlier than in the big cities].

Toni: I always thought that was because it was next to all those other buildings—burning down the synagogue was a risk to them.

Wally: One of the older women from Roth told us this story years later: The guy next door pleaded with them not to burn the synagogue because his house would be affected. And they were going to chop down the pillars. He pleaded with them and that's when they stated "we're going to use it as a storage place." But the people who came to destroy the synagogue weren't from the village. There were a couple of people early on, a couple of women who objected, but they were arrested. God knows what happened to them. They had to have been about 35, 36 years old and they were put in jail by the active Nazis—these women were attacked.

Wally: Do you remember going to school?

Toni: Oh yes. I started when I was six in 1904. There was the old school house and then they built a new school house. The old school house was unused at least up until we left Germany. It was in front of your father's house in Roth.

Wally: That was torn down the last time I was there.

Toni: Well, it was there when we left Germany.

Wally: So, the new school was where I went to school. You went to school there too?

Toni: Yes.

Wally: How many children were there in the school?

Toni: I would estimate the big class was more than twenty. The other class was not as big. There were eight grades.

Wally: All together in one room?

Toni: No, there were two rooms.

Wally: Who was your teacher?

Toni: Herr Wagner.

Wally: My goodness, he was my teacher too. You mean to tell me he was there from 1904 and was there in 1934 too, thirty years later?

Toni: I didn't know if he was there in the first years. But he was there during my last years in school.

Wally: He taught everything; arithmetic, history, everything?

Toni: I think everything.

Wally: What time did you go to school in the morning?

Toni: I don't know if it was eight or nine.

Wally: And then did you eat lunch in school or did you go home?

Toni: We could go home. Sometimes we brought lunch with us.

Wally: How long did the school last?

Toni: I think we had "second breakfast" there in school and went home for lunch. In the morning school lasted until twelve, and after lunch I think it was from one to three, and then continued for an hour after for recess for sports or games.

Wally: You didn't use a notebook in the early days. Didn't you use a slate and a slate pencil?

Toni: They were called a *tafel* and a *griffel*.

Wally: What did you erase with?

Toni: Water and a *shwam* (a sponge.)

Wally: Did you write with a regular pencil and paper too?

Toni: Yes, in the book. Sure, sure.

Wally: What did you study?

Toni: I never studied. You didn't study in such a school. We didn't have books or other study materials to take home like they do these days.

Wally: Did you do arithmetic?

Toni: Yes. And writing. And reading.

Wally: Do you remember what you read?

Toni: Don't ask me; it was a few years ago. (laughs)

Wally: I know. (laughs) I don't remember what I read either. What about religious studies?

Toni: When they had religion the Jewish kids weren't there. We weren't even in the school; it was usually in the morning, the first class. And we came late—we didn't have to go.

Wally: Do you remember how many Jewish children there were in school?

Toni: Not many; maybe twelve at most.

Wally: Who were they? Did your brothers go to the same school?

Toni: Yes, they did. And I was in class with your mother, Selma, and her brother, as well the children of our former landlords, the Bergensteins and the Nathans. Joseph Bergenstein, that was the son.

Wally: What about all of your other cousins in the town? Weren't there a bunch of them?

Toni: No, none of them were school anymore. Selma and I were nine years younger than then next youngest cousin, so they were not in school anymore when we went.

Wally: When you were in school, did you play with the other children too? The Gentiles?

Toni: Yes, yes. After school we came out and were playing together.

Wally: There were never any problems that you can remember in the early years?

Toni: No. Maybe they made... what is the name?

Wally: Remarks?

Toni: Yes, that happened sometimes.

Wally: How do you know? Do you remember any?

Toni: I seem to remember the remarks were made, but nothing specific. I have forgotten a lot.

Wally: Sure, we all do. It's wonderful that you remember so much though. Go ahead; tell me a little something about the life in Roth when you were young.

Toni: On Friday night if no one would come over to visit, we went to bed early. Then came the girl who turned off the lights and we went to bed, and the next morning the girl came and made the coffee.

Wally: Who was the girl?

Toni: In English I think you would say maid or a servant. She would come over on Friday and Saturday to do things we couldn't because we were observing the Sabbath.

Wally: You paid her or what?

Toni: Yes, and she helped us around the house. You know, when you were very young, Selma and your father had a live-in gentile servant who was mostly a babysitter for you kids. I think Anna was her name.

Wally: Was she there when you married my father? I was so young I really don't remember her.

Toni: Oh no, she was gone. After the Nuremburg laws were passed, Gentiles couldn't work for the Jews and Anna had to leave.

Wally: What did you usually do in the evening?

Toni: Knitting or reading; there was not a thing to do.

Wally: Did the men play cards a lot?

Toni: Not during the week; during the weekend and Sunday afternoon. I remember my father went with the rest to watch when they played cards, but he didn't play cards.

Wally: When did you go to study Hebrew and prayers?

Toni: Every week. The teacher came to us. Every month it was in another house.

Wally: What was the name of the Hebrew teacher you had?

Toni: Josef Sweitch. He came from Gladenbach. He was Polish.

Wally: He was probably Orthodox, no? Very religious?

Toni: Yes, I think so. And you had a different teacher growing up.

Wally: Yes, *Lehrer* (teacher) Simon. I later found out he was killed by the Nazis in Auschwitz. He was also from Poland, wasn't he?

Toni: Yes. He was even more religious than my teacher. He didn't like to eat with us. Even though he knew we had a kosher house yet he didn't eat anything from us. And when there was a bar mitzvah or something that he came to, he brought his own soup and bread.

Wally: Did you go travelling at all when you were a child that you can remember?

Toni: Yes, to Borken and to Kirchhain [to visit relatives]. And I went to school in the city of Marburg. I went to trade and sewing school when I was 16 years old. Selma, your mother, was at the school in Marburg with me. Then when I was 17, I went to business school in the city of Giessen.

Wally: Did you go to school with Selma's brother Herman too?

Toni: Oh, yes, sure, the village school in Roth. He was a year older than me.

Wally: What happened to Herman?

Toni: At eighteen years he was dead. It's a shame. He went off to WWI, fighting for the German army. He was killed in Macedonia, fighting the French.

Wally: Were there any other Jewish boys from the village killed in the First World War?

Toni: Yes. My old landlord Josef Bergenstein. But he maybe was not from Roth, maybe the village across the river. And your cousin Berthold [Otto's father] got wounded. He was in the army along with your father and your father's two brothers. You know, your father, Markus, was an *unterofficer*, a corporal. Berthold was an interpreter for the barracks, translating French to German. He was wounded near his shoulder. It was a hole on the arm. It happened in France. He came back wounded and was taken care of. He was sent to the Schweitz (Switzerland) for treatment under some exchange agreement. Switzerland was neutral back then too—the Germans would send their wounded to the Swiss for rehabilitation. My uncle and my aunt went there to visit him. And Berthold was engaged at that time to cousin Otto's mother, Clara. Clara went to Frankfurt to see if she could join Berthold's parents in visiting him. But she was unable to get a visa to go to Switzerland. I remember I was at this time going to the business school in Giessen. I was supposed to go on the train home with Clara after she returned from visiting Berthold, but that never happened. It was so sad, she was packed to go but they didn't let her go.

Wally: What did Berthold do when he came back?

Toni: He worked in his father's business, selling dry goods. When Berthold was young, people suggested to my uncle that he should be sent to university. My uncle said, "No, it's the only boy I have. He has to stay in the business." So he didn't send Berthold to university. It wasn't right.

Wally: But Berthold was quite educated?

Toni: Oh yes, but from reading. He was a very smart man. He could also read Hebrew. He could even read from the Torah. So could Berthold's brother-in-law. Family of smart men they were.

Wally: Who else read from the Torah?

Toni: There were a number of men who could, and always the *parnes*. That was the elder or leader of the Jewish community locally. All the villages had one. There were two during the time I was in Roth. The first was a very smart, well-respected man, Herz Höxter.

The second was his son-in-law, Herman Höchster; he actually lived next to us when I married your father. I know that he was arrested on Kristallnacht.

Wally: You said the first *parnes* was well-respected, but nothing like that about the second? I thought he was a smart man too.

Toni: Oh, he was dumb as a cow.

Wally: Really? I thought he was a really smart guy.

Toni: He married a woman that was not well; she had TB and that's why he was not so smart.

Wally: So he was dumb?

Toni: Well from an education standpoint he was smart, but when he came to choosing a wife, he was not smart.

Wally: His wife was Herz Höxter's daughter?

Toni: Yes. Matilda. She was the one with TB.

Wally: How come the father in law and son in law had the same name?

Toni: I don't know. They didn't write it the same way. One was H-Ö-X-T-E-R and then the other was H-Ö-C-H-S-T-E-R. Sounded the same, but spelled differently. They're all *mishpucha*, related. Most of the Jewish families in the local villages in a given region were related. Even you and I are related to both the Höxters and Höchsters.

Wally: What was your father's father's name? I don't remember what it was, but it seemed so exotic to me.

Toni: Bonfang? Bonfang Stern. His name came from my great

grandmother, Miriam Bonfang, who was probably of French descent. Bonfang was given his mother's surname as a first name. He worked with his brother Haune, your mother Selma's grandfather. And they had a lot of sisters. They had one in Alsfeld. They had one in Gladenbach. I don't remember where the others lived. But I talked to all of them when I was young. Sadly both Bonfang and Haune died suddenly.

Wally: They caught a disease, didn't they?

Toni: Oh yes, it was smallpox. They went to a funeral and one of them caught it. They went to Oberweimar for a funeral and took part in the *tahara* (ritual washing of the body of the deceased). I think that was the place where one of them got sick and died and the other brother got it a few days later. Such strong men they were. They were about forty when they died.

Wally: The wives ran the business after their husbands died, right?

Toni: Yes.

Wally: That must have been a terrible thing. Do you remember much about them?

Toni: Only very little... The old mailman was talking about it once. He said that they were very good. They were nice people, these two brothers. That's what the old man told me.

[Wally: In 1997 my brother Herb wrote and distributed to family members a history/memoir of the Stern family in Roth. Here is his account of Haune and Bonfang's story:

Herz [Stern] married Miriam Bonfang of Lohra in 1815. She was the daughter of an old Jewish family whose lineage went back to the Thirty Years War, when her ancestors settled in Amoeneburg. They had nine children, seven daughters and two sons.... Herz died at the age of 54 and was survived by his widow Miriam, his sons Haune and Bonfang, and daughters Bertha, Esther and Lea.... In 1855 Haune married Adelheid Wetzstein from Treis and two years later [Adelheid's] sister Malchen, married Bonfang.... In February of 1868, Haune and Bonfang died suddenly. The story that has down through the generations is that the brother had attended a tahara (a ritual preparing the body for burial) and they were infected with a fatal disease. The year 1886 must have been a year of horror for Adelheid. She was pregnant with a son who died four months later [and] had five other children.... The fate of her sister Malchen was similar. She was left with four children ages 2 to 10. But these were strong women they supported each other and jointly managed the family. Very likely they limited their activities to sale of dry goods and food products.... My grandfather Herz was only two years old when his father [Haune] died.... He was married in 1895 to Emma [Esther] Rothschild from Angerod.... Herz and Emma had two children: Herman born in 1898, and Selma (my mother), born in 1899.]

Wally: What about your grandmother Malchen, Bonfang's wife?

Toni: She lived to be seventy four or five. I was maybe eight or nine years old when she died.

Wally: Do you have good memories from her?

Toni: Yes, she was a nice woman. But she didn't work anymore when I remember her. No. Not like the people, not like they work now. I think of her always sitting in a chair and peeling potatoes. She washed the cups and saucers but not the other dishes. They couldn't be washed in the living room but the other dishes were washed in the kitchen. And maybe she mended stockings; it's possible.

She did this, otherwise nothing. When she wanted, my grandmother would let Berta cook for her. And when the food was finished, then Berta brought it to my grandmother and she had to taste it to see if it had the right taste. It was not that Berta didn't know how to taste it herself. She wanted to be nice to her so that she'd say "but it needs something more on the food!" (laughs)

Wally: What about your other grandmother? Did she live with you?

Toni: No, she lived by my uncle in his house, or she was supposed to. Well, that was her house. She had the *sitzheit* (similar to life estate) in this house. The people made this when they were young; that the young people get the house but the old person has the right to have a room in the house as long as she is alive.

Wally: The son got the house but he had to promise that the mother could live in it?

Toni: It was in writing.

Wally: In writing that the mother could live in the house as long as she's alive?

Toni: It was in the law that the young people had to do what was right and decent for her.

Wally: That was their obligation?

Toni: Yes.

Wally: And when she died, everything belonged to the son?

Toni: Yes. And he had to take care of the funeral and everything right away.

Wally: You told me once you were there when your grandmother [Malchen] died.

Toni: Yes, I didn't know that she was sick. I didn't have any idea. She was in bed; lying in bed. And then around evening she got very sick and died. I didn't have any idea that she was even sick.

Wally: Did they have a doctor?

Toni: I don't know… I believe so. Once in a while the doctor came.

Wally: When a Jew died in one of the local villages what happened?

Toni: The body stayed in the house until the funeral.

Wally: And then they washed the body, didn't they?

Toni: Yes. It was a ritual. Though it was dangerous having the body at the home because of diseases - that was how Bonfang and his brother got sick.

Wally: Who normally did the washing?

Toni: They had women who volunteered for that. Sometimes close male family members would assist, the way Bonfang did.

Wally: Did you ever participate?

Toni: Once my mother wanted me to come with. But it was not for me so I never went a second time. My mother never said anything because I didn't want to be around the bodies.

Wally: And the coffin? Who would make a coffin?

Toni: They made it themselves, the Jews. The *schreiner* (cabinet maker) would cut the wood as big as they wanted and the Jews would put it together.

Wally: They did that until the Nuremberg laws right? I remember at my grandmother's funeral [Emma, mother of Selma] in 1937, after the laws were passed, that the coffin was poorly made and it leaked because it was poorly constructed.

Toni: When the Gentiles couldn't make the coffins for us, the Jews had to do it themselves. We didn't know about cutting and making the joints. We didn't have the skills necessary, but we got by to the best of our abilities.

Wally: Yes. So, when you were growing up, did they carry the coffin to the cemetery or did they have a wagon?

Toni: It was always on a wagon. And the people walked behind it.

Wally: Cousin Otto said to me once that in the old days they used to have people sing at the funeral. I think that Otto said that about his father Berthold's funeral because he used to sing in the choir and therefore the people of the choir came to sing at the funeral.

Toni: I don't remember that. But sometimes there was a choir. You know, Otto's father was a good singer. He had a voice that was completely different. He had a beautiful voice. His children took their mother's voice though.

Wally: Tell me something about my maternal grandfather, Herz Stern [Selma's father].

Toni: He was the youngest of all the children I think.

Wally: What happened to his brothers and sisters? Do you remember any of them?

Toni: Oh, sure. There were a bunch of girls and one other boy. They lived all over the area—none in Roth but all nearby. There was one sister who lived in Josbach who was so old fashioned and stingy. I never saw something like this. Terrible.

Wally: I remember one of grandfather Herz's sisters married and moved to another town. She had a son, Charles Hammersley, who lives in Chicago now.

Toni: He was Charles Hammerschlag back in Germany.

Wally: And they were all very Orthodox I would imagine?

Toni: Those people were all Orthodox. Except one family who lived in the village Treis. They ate from one pot and we didn't eat like that. And they ate parts of the meat we didn't eat.

Wally: Who did the slaughtering in Roth?

Toni: It was the *parnes*. The *parnes* always did the slaughtering.

Wally: I remember that my grandfather, Herz, would sometimes assist in the slaughtering of kosher meat. I watched it once, it made me sick to my stomach. He did it in the yard of our house.

Toni: Speaking of your grandfather reminds me that I wanted to say something about your grandmother Emma—Herz's wife. Her family name was Rothschild. She came from Angerod.

Wally: She must have come to Roth about the same time that Berta came to Roth.

Toni: I wanted to say that Emma loved you dearly. She was a fine person. She went to school and they learned something that was more than could be learned in a small town. Emma had no mother. Her mother died when she was very young. A mother watches over the children so that they learn something. Emma didn't have that guidance, but she was well grounded even though they were big talkers in her family. She knew to keep the house in order and was not dumb. Her brothers, I don't know what they were or why, but they talked so much. But she was not a dumb woman, your grandmother. No, no.

Wally: Was Berta particularly close to her?

Toni: Oh, absolutely. They were close. Berta's mother Adelheid was still alive and so was Emma's. We all visited often in the house. She was a fine lady, that Emma. Adelheid too.

Wally: Do you remember any of Emma's family?

Toni: Oh yes. One's name was Flora.

Wally: Flora… I met her once. She's still alive [in 1988, when this conversation took place]. She lives in Israel. You know, I told you. And there was Sigmund in Haifa. I met him the first time I went to Israel. He had a store.

Toni: Sure, yeah, I remember. He was very religious.

Wally: Very religious. Still was in Israel. When I was there I stayed with him over *Sukkot*. I slept under the stars in his *sukkah*.

Toni: Their whole family was religious.

Wally: But there's another Rothschild who's still alive; he's a doctor, a psychiatrist. And I seem to recall there's another one who's a dentist.

Toni: They had a big family.

Wally: They lived in Rishon L'Zion, a small town near Tel Aviv. They went there in the mid-1930s. I think most of the family got out of Germany and headed there during that time.

Toni: That sounds right, but there was one sister who moved to England.

Wally: You once told me about when your cousin Paula got married. Do you remember that?

Toni: The wedding was in Marburg. It was when I was a child, maybe eleven or twelve. I wanted to sell flower baskets. Nobody bought them and then I gave Paula one of these baskets at her wedding.

Wally: Were there a lot of people there?

Toni: Not compared to what there is now at weddings.

Wally: No? How many people do you think? Fifty?

Toni: There were not fifty, maybe forty. I don't know anymore. People didn't invite so many people then.

Wally: And then Paula moved to Kirchhain? [Kirchhain was a much larger village that had a Jewish seminary. Among others, the philosopher Leo Strauss studied there in his youth.]

Toni: It was nice; a small town. I would go there by train. It took maybe an hour from Roth. We had to change trains in Lollar. I was more patient then and my village was fairly little compared to Kirchhain. Clara Hammerschlag, your mother's cousin Clara from Treis—Meta's sister—married a man named Wertheim from Kirchhain. Our cousins the Bachenheimers [Ida and Emanuel] also lived there for a while. They came from Rauischholzhausen. They had a beautiful house in Kirchhain. I think someone else started it and couldn't finish it. They didn't have the money to finish and the Bachenheimers finished it. [The Bachenheimers left Germany before the war and also came to Chicago.]

Toni's Marriage to Markus

Toni: Let's talk about some of what you remember growing up. Perhaps starting with before I married your father.

Wally: Well my mother Selma passed away in Germany when I was five, and I was not allowed to go to the funeral.

Toni: Well, I have to say to you, Wally, that although it's very different, your father and I didn't allow your little sister, Helen, to go to your bar mitzvah in Chicago. The youngsters were just not considered part of the adult family.

Wally: Did Herb go to my bar mitzvah? I remember he went to the funeral in Germany.

Toni: Yes, of course he went, but he was older.

Wally: Is part of the reason that the children were not permitted to such events because they would probably misbehave?

Toni: That may have been a part of it... Do you remember how your mother got sick?

Wally: All of us—this is back in 1934, I guess—caught colds or the flu or whatever it was and became sick. Selma also got sick. There were no doctors locally, you know. We didn't have a doctor. Finally, when she was really sick, high fever, they took her to the Jewish section of the hospital in Marburg. I think it was diagnosed as blood poisoning.

Toni: It was pneumonia.

Wally: Yes, I heard later it was pneumonia, you know, which they didn't diagnose properly. And she died very quickly at the age of thirty-four. It was never told to me that she had died. The only thing that I do remember was sudden dread in the house. Dad was not there. And they mentioned something and then, Emma, Selma's mother, who was not that well herself, was very upset. And then I remember some relatives came the next day... Max Wertheim, a cousin of my mother. And Marga Bachenheimer.

Toni: Where was Herb?

Wally: Well, he probably was around, but I don't remember him being at the hospital. He was older and I didn't necessarily understand what was going on. I was overwhelmed and confused and looking back, it was a very solitary experience for a young boy of my age.

What I do remember clearly was when Dad came home from the hospital. I remember he took us aside to a separate room and I sat on his lap and Irene was the other side, and Herb was there, too, and he told us our mother had died. Whatever that meant. And oh, I remember crying and everyone else was crying too. But that was the end of the discussion, no further discussion. The next morning was the funeral. Anna, the maid, stayed with me at the house. We met her later, many years later when we she came to our reunion in 1984. But she worked for us for several years, and when the Nuremberg laws were passed, I think in '35, she had to leave. So anyway, she was there. She took care of me. I remember being with her and the next morning, a wagon came up with a coffin on it and people walking behind it. I stood in the door with Anna. Everybody walked to the cemetery. But there was no discussion and I wasn't allowed to go. Even though they walked right by.

Toni: Well, you were five years old. Do you remember if your older sister Irene went?

Wally: I think Irene went.

Toni: Well, I suppose that makes sense—she was only a year younger than Herb.

Wally: Years later my Christian neighbor told me that I went to her house and sat on her lap for hours and cried during the funeral and the shiva afterwards. She said I used to come over quite a bit—that's probably true. I have good memories of going there, you know I was only five years old—she was a nice lady who always told me how much she liked Selma.

Toni: Did your father ever talk to you about the funeral afterwards?

Wally: Never talked about it again, none of it. And I knew my grandmother, Emma, was not well. I slept downstairs at the time. She slept on the side next to the furnace—next to our stove. I slept on the other side as a young child. And I don't know why that was—I can't give you a reason for that. Grandfather slept on the sofa away from grandmother. Maybe it was because Dad had the bedroom upstairs. Along the lines of me not being invited to big family events, I wasn't invited to your wedding to Dad either.

Toni: We got married in Marburg at a Jewish restaurant. I think it was Strauss restaurant. You may not have been invited, but others couldn't make it. I remember some cousins couldn't come at the last moment. They had to flee their town, Nieder-Ohmen, because of the anti-Semitism. After our marriage we saw less of the family—it became much harder to travel.

Wally: I remember Grandpa Jonas, Dad's father, rarely came to visit, especially after Selma died. Even though he lived nearby with Uncle Jacob, I saw him infrequently. When Uncle Jacob moved to Palestine, I remember seeing Grandpa once more when Jacob was packing up, but after that Grandpa Jonas moved to Frankfurt and I never saw him again. He couldn't get a visa to go to Palestine, so he ended up in Frankfurt, yet we never saw him. It must have been hard for him to travel back and forth as a Jew.

Toni: Well, it may not have been completely due to troubles with Jews traveling in Germany.

Wally: What do you mean?

Toni: I disliked him.

Wally: Why? Was he not nice to you?

Toni: He treated his wife badly.

Wally: But you had no problem with Selma's parents, right?

Toni: No, I loved Emma and her husband Herz. Once your father and I married, we were all living in the house. In the same house together.

Wally: OK. I was young and didn't understand family dynamics that well. So you moved into the house with everyone and it was all right? Everyone got along?

Toni: Yes, I always had a good relationship with Emma and Herz. And it was nice having them around, especially since my father had died a few years earlier—in 1933, the same year Hitler came to power.

Wally: And Berta lived several houses down from us anyway, right?

Toni: Yes, she lived there with my brothers, Hugo and Louis.

Wally: I remember I liked Hugo. But your other brother, Louis, I hardly knew because he was in Frankfurt so much of the time.

Toni: Oh yes, he was quite busy with his business; he worked in one of these clothing stores, you know.

Wally: Did Berta and her sons always live in that house or did they move into the house on our block when you married Dad?

Toni: They just always lived nearby, but I don't think that Berta was a favorite with you and your brother.

Wally: She was very strict. She was very bossy but it must have been very tough for her. Cousin Otto once told me that when Selma lay dying, that she asked Berta to take care of us children.

Toni: That's not surprising—after all we were all related.

Wally: Yeah, we were related but not through Berta. Through her husband, your grandfather.

Toni: I don't remember if it was Selma or Berta that asked that me to take care of you, but it just sort of happened.

Toni: So back to the wedding. I don't think Herb was invited there, either, but I'm not sure. And I will always remember the first time I came into the house as your father's wife, there was an incident. Initially you and I did not get along very well.

Wally: Oh, I remember that incident distinctly. I was playing by the fireplace in the living room with some cards, and Father and you strolled in from the wedding—he must have said something like "this is your mother." Something like that. I gave him a glare and exclaimed "you're a *misgebot*." You know what that means?

Toni: Of course, it means "You're a bastard."

Wally: And Dad grabbed my cards and he slapped me. Only time I ever remember him hitting me. He slapped me and took my cards and threw them into the fireplace. They were the only cards I ever had. And I never played cards again.

Toni: Oh, goodness, I never realized that was the reason you didn't like cards.

Wally: It was terrible.

Toni: Yes, I remember there was a period of time I don't think we talked to each other after that. But we eventually became closer and did a lot of things together, definitely before we left for America.

Getting the Affidavits

Wally: Where did we get our affidavits to come to the US? What part of the family did it come from?

Toni: It was on Berta's side of the family. The affidavits came from one of Berta's great nephews, Moritz Rosenbusch.

Wally: So that side of the family must have left Germany early then?

Toni: Yes. Berta's nephew, Levy, Mortiz's father, went to America when he was seventeen. There was a relative that wanted to take him along and so he went. It was probably around the turn of the century. Moritz's father settled in the states and started a family. Moritz and his siblings were quite successful. I think there were five in total—Moritz and his brother, plus two or three sisters. They lived in Kokomo, Indiana. Moritz's father married a nice Jewish woman in America. Moritz married a Catholic woman, yet he still got us the affidavits. You know, Moritz gave some of my other relatives an affidavit too.

Wally: Who was that? Who were these relatives?

Toni: Bella—they moved to Maryland, to Baltimore.

Wally: I met her once. She had glaucoma, remember?

Toni: A short while ago she was here in Chicago. There was a bar mitzvah and she was here to visit. But I was by your brother Herbert, and I wasn't here to see her. She is 85 and she drives a car still. Strong woman.

Wally: You know, I think a lot about our affidavits. Were it not for you, I can only think of what would have happened to me and my father, and my brother and sister. We were saved by people who we didn't know, who were *your* relatives. We had never met them before. It's ironic that with the tragedy of my mother's premature passing, my father was fortunate enough to marry you. And that enabled all of us to escape as a family. I don't ever remember meeting Moritz or thanking him. You met him once you said, didn't you?

Toni: Yes, he came to Chicago, but he stayed by other relatives. We didn't talk much—there was very little connection since they didn't speak German and I wasn't confident in my English then. But I will always be grateful to him. It was unfortunate, when we got here we had no connection with them. I don't know how much later after we got here, but he arranged a party so that we could see his mother and father, who were still alive. But a short time after it was planned, she died. So the party was called off.

Wally: And you never heard from him again?

Toni: No. He couldn't write and we couldn't write. Later he died because he got sick. I don't know what was wrong with him. His father died of cancer; maybe he had the same but he had children who are still around. Berta and I wrote so many letters to family and friends in the States back when we were in Germany and he was the one who helped us. He put in so much work to get the paperwork and guarantees together, and we never even had a real conversation. Such a kind man.

Wally: Of course Father also tried to contact people that he knew of in the United States. But he didn't succeed in getting a visa through these contacts. I've also pondered why my father did not try to follow the example of his brother Jacob—but of course he didn't have the money.

Toni: Jacob [Markus' brother] from Nieder-Ohmen—he moved to Israel, right?

Wally: He was able to purchase a farm in Palestine in a *moshav,* Ramat Hadar, near Tel Aviv. It wasn't Israel yet. He had to sell his house in Nieder-Ohmen. He was the oldest son, so he and his family lived in his parents' house with my grandparents. Selling his house apparently gave him enough money to pay for passage to Palestine.

[Wally: Markus's father Jonas Roth lived in Nieder-Ohmen, an hour's train ride from Roth. The oldest son, Jacob was married to Setta; they had two daughters, Ilse and Gertrude. By 1935 the entire

household was under intense anti-Semitic pressure. Jonas was threatened and forced to leave Nieder-Ohmen. He fled to Frankfort. Jacob, the oldest son, became the owner of the house. Jacob learned of the so-called Transfer Agreement. He was able to sell the house for one thousand English pounds. Together with money he already had, this enabled him to purchase a five dunam plot of land in the *moshav* (small farming village) of Ramat Hadar, a few miles from Tel Aviv. In 1936 Jacob, Setta, and Ilse were able to go to Palestine and settle on this land. Their other daughter Gertrude married in 1936 and emigrated to Tel Aviv.

The Transfer Agreement, a highly controversial arrangement between Nazi German authorities and authorities in Palestine (Jewish as well as British), permitted German Jews to transfer their capital when emigrating to Palestine provided that they use some of the money to purchase German goods. It was estimated by some authorities that nearly thirty thousand German Jews were able to leave Germany for Palestine under the Transfer Agreement.]

Toni: Jacob's mother had died earlier in the 1930s and his father died in Frankfurt soon after Jacob left.

Wally: Well, why didn't you and Dad explore the possibility of Shanghai or South Africa, didn't some other neighbors end up there?

Toni: Money. It took a lot of money. Money to travel. Money to get a visa. Money to start over when you arrived. And that was only if the Nazis would let you leave with money.

Wally: I remember that we did have some money with us when we left. We hid money in the bottom of a coffee pot. That coffee pot is still in the family.

STARTING OVER IN CHICAGO

The next part of the dialogue concerns our lives once we were in Chicago. I include some events which are difficult to write about. I feel that it is important to include the special struggles that both my father Markus and my sister Irene experienced in this country and the sad circumstances of their deaths. I have a sense that I owe this to their memories since as a family we have not spoken a great deal about their deaths.

Wally: So I wanted you to talk about your relationship with Dad once we were in America. It's still amazing to me that no one ever told Helen this about our family.

Toni: What do you mean?

Wally: About Selma. And how you were not my mother, or Herb or Irene's mother. There was some kind of a…a curtain or whatever you call it—that this was not something to be talked about. It reminded me of my mother's funeral and all the confusion that surrounded that for me.

Toni: What? Because Helen didn't know that you had a different mother.

Wally: Oh yes, absolutely. But we didn't talk about a lot of things.

Toni: I just never saw the point of making a fuss. I loved you children all, as my own.

Wally: Helen once told me that one of our relatives stayed with us while her parents came to pick me up in New York. Apparently this niece mentioned she thought that our family was very silent, like a prison—almost repressive. And I look at this, like a lack of speaking about Selma ever, and that's what she meant by repressive, I think. I also didn't talk about my mother Selma's death.

Toni: Right.

Wally: I mean, if it came up I would tell people, but it rarely did. You know? But I never said to Dad, "well, tell me about this or tell me about, you know, when you first married Selma," you know? I look at this in contrast to Helen, who had a conversation like that with her son. He asked her about her first husband who died shortly after they married. She told her son all about it very openly.

Toni: Your father wouldn't have spoken about it. Not even he and I talked about it.

Wally: Well, we finally talked about it toward the end. He told me a little bit about what happened.

Toni: When did you figure out that Helen didn't know?

Wally: I remember when she was in middle school, she had to do a family roots project for school. I talked to her one day after classes, and she seemed quite surprised.

Toni: In grade school?

Wally: The Ray school. She said she was writing an autobiography. It traced who you were. And that's when she found out that you were not my mother, and that you were not Irene's mother, and that you were not Herbert's mother. She obviously hadn't known that.

When I talked to her she said she was in shock. It was such a shock and apparently only exacerbated when she saw pictures. You know those pictures of me and Selma?

Toni: Well, we never had any pictures of Selma out in our home. But I remember the picture you're talking about—it's the one with you on Selma's lap. I showed it to her, probably for that project. At first Helen thought it was me. The picture has Irene on one side and Herb on the other with you in Selma's lap. I guess nobody would have ever told her different if we hadn't had that conversation. And she only learned about it because she had to ask these questions for school anyway.

Wally: Helen told me she was amazed that I never told her and Herb never told her.

Toni: Selma and I, we had the same name, too, our maiden name was Stern. And we were cousins. I had an interest in keeping the family together. No need to cause trouble. But also I did not want to talk about this. You must be able to see the discomfort in a conversation about that should it go the wrong way.

Wally: Well, I imagine it would be awkward to say you married Father in part at the urging of Berta because she made a promise to Selma to take care of us kids.

Toni: Yes, but I also wanted to marry your father. Still, I was nervous, I didn't know how to handle this topic. Your father would have helped with the conversation.

Wally: Did Helen get a chance to learn more about the family and our lives back in Germany later on?

Toni: Yes. For example, we used to come home after services at the Hyde Park Liberal Congregation, on 53rd and Blackstone, and sit and talk.

Wally: Right. We used to come back after Kol Nidre services. There was one light on. You were allowed to have one light on, and I remember that there were these little sheets of toilet paper that were torn in the bathroom so you wouldn't have to tear the toilet paper. And we did not do that for Shabbat, but we did it on Kol Nidre. And we would sit, and I think it was in the dining room, it wouldn't have been the kitchen—that would have been wrong on Kol Nidre, sitting in the kitchen. And we would talk about what it was like when they had Kol Nidre in Germany.

Toni: That's when Helen got to learn all these things about people who were our family from back in Germany—stories about Otto Stern, his mother Clara and others. All these stories that would come out at these times and Helen thought that was the only way she was going to find out what was really going on in the family

Wally: What were your first memories of Dad once he got to America?

Toni: Oh, my first memories of your father? Well, let's see. I remember your father was a very warm man in Roth. He was liked by everyone, and I don't ever remember him losing his temper with anyone, well except when you children misbehaved. But I don't think I have the same memories of him once we arrived in Chicago. Actually, I know I don't have the same memories. I didn't mean to be a complainer about that. I feel that he became a little bit... distant.

Wally: And he surely didn't take any interest in our schooling.

Toni: Oh, no. Well, he didn't want Herb to go to college, and he definitely didn't want Helen to go to college. I don't think she would have gone to college were it not for you and Herb.

Wally: I agree.

Toni: I remember Helen told me that she was going to try to enroll at the University of Chicago and they had an entrance exam that she hoped to pass. It was such a strange requirement to me that I didn't know what to say. She said she would go to the University of Illinois at Navy Pier if she wasn't accepted to Chicago. She had a plan, well two plans!

Wally: Back to Dad, so you don't remember him being warm?

Toni: As I said, there was a difference between Markus in Roth and Markus in Chicago. And I think that sort of defines the way he was once he got here. I think coming to this country was an enormous shock. That's not to say he didn't show signs of his personality from Roth; his warmth would come out every so often, such as when he saw friends.

Wally: Do you remember any of his friends?

Toni: Well, there were a few groups; the Jewish people from the stockyards where he worked, and then there were relatives, and also people from Germany—some were family and some were other refugees.

Wally: Yes. Who else?

Toni: I remember your father talking to the Bachenheimers on Saturday mornings after synagogue. Helen always thought your father didn't like them so much. She said it was jealousy because they had a store. I think that's what he always wanted for himself—to have a store that he could run with his oldest son.

Wally: What about Joseph?

Toni: Oh yes, Joseph Stern from Nieder-Ohmen. He and your father were in the German army together. And he had a daughter, Ruth Stern. I thought that you and she were going to get married.

Wally: That's right. They lived on the old West Side when I dated Ruth. I took her home on the El twice—that neighborhood scared me in those days. It was towards the Maxwell Street area.

Toni: You know, your father was very friendly with Joseph Stern. And when he let himself be friendly, he loved talking to people. But he had no social life at that time. And I think he didn't have the energy for a social life. He went to work at five in the morning, came home at five in the afternoon, and it was all physical labor. I don't know how far he had to go or how many times he had to change buses or street cars to get to work.

Wally: I remember, it was twice. He changed buses twice. Socially, he never played cards either, which he did in Germany.

Toni: In the beginning he was too tired. It was hard. He didn't have time. I remember he once said to Otto's mother, in German, that it was easier *over there*. The butcher business was different. He had to get up early in the morning and came home too late. He started early and then he was very tired. He didn't play cards.

Wally: What kind of cards did they play in Germany?

Toni: Sixty six or skat.

Wally: Did you play?

Toni: No, I didn't play. But people should play when they are young. Then when they are old, playing cards is nice. For me, it's good that you get to meet people here playing cards. I don't get so lonely. If I have nothing to do, then I sleep or watch television. It was a quiet life that people got used to.

Wally: What worried you most about Dad?

Toni: His health was poor and he worked so hard. I was always worried about him. I was constantly, constantly worried about him.

That he should sleep, and that he should not eat salt. He couldn't eat salt.

Wally: High blood pressure, that's right.

Toni: I tried to help him keep to his diet. But of course, I wasn't such a stickler because he needed to have some pleasures. A small cake never hurt anyone.

Wally: From the outside, it was a very limited, I thought, life for him and that's how I saw it. I was living out of the house because I was an adult by that point. I remember Helen, who grew up in the house with you and Dad in Chicago saying that as she got older, much older, when she brought friends over to the house, he was much friendlier and was much warmer and could kid with people. I always took that for granted because I remember Dad in a certain way from Germany. But to Helen, it was such a surprise. She found him volatile. You and I don't remember him losing his temper... Helen remembers him losing his temper a lot.

Toni: Against who?

Wally: Well, it probably started with Irene. But Helen remembers being in the house when he would get mad at you. He would get mad at me. He would get mad at Herb. She remembers that. But I can't tell you what it was about.

Toni: He got mad at you?

Wally: I'm trying to remember the specifics. I don't really recall, but Helen felt so strongly. I think that in part it shows how he related less with Helen as a child an adult. She was closer to him by the time she was college age than she was during the first ten years of her life.

Toni: Well, there were lots of fears he had. We feared that we were not going to be able to stay in that apartment because it was becoming too expensive, that was after the war when rent control went away. We didn't know what they were going to charge us and your father made little money—he made $45 or $48 a week, maybe less—at least he was union. I remember him counting out the money in the little yellow envelopes. I could never figure out if we were safe with money.

Wally: Do you remember Dad bringing home meat? During the war? When meat was being rationed? Did Dad ever make sausage?

Toni: Yes, but always with non-kosher meat. So he would keep it in the basement. He was working in the stockyards—there were opportunities to get small pieces of meat. I know there was one place where we got corned beef. They made pretty good corned beef. And he brought tongue. And, you children ate it. Your father and I did not because it wasn't kosher. We fed it to you on the back porch, never upstairs. Meat was rationed and very hard to come by during the war. Your father took whatever meat they would give him. They had big gray vats with the bits of leftover meat.

Wally: I remember some sort of grinding machine; I remember working the grinder. By the end of the war I loved tongue. I still love it to this day. I guess at the time it was a delicacy.

Toni: Herb liked tongue too. But Irene didn't. It was a sore subject with your father.

Wally: What do you remember of Father in the synagogue?

Toni: Congregation Habonim; it was a congregation of German refugees in Hyde Park. I remember he used to always sit in the same place. He would go early. Helen and I would come later. He would sit in the same place on the side. I don't remember him having any relationship with the rabbi. There was a Men's Club, but he was not a member.

Wally: I always thought that he felt, because he had no money, that he couldn't make any contributions. Remember that?

Toni: Do you know what I remember? Honors cost money. Aliyahs cost money. Money we didn't have.

Wally: Yeah, members who gave contributions would pay to get the honor of being called to the Torah. And then the Rabbi would even call out the names of those who gave as well as their contribution amounts as they came up to the *bimah*—$10, $25, more....

Toni: No, and that was awful. It was awful. When they called you for an aliyah, you had made a pledge. So the right person, $100? But Dad had no money. And so they didn't call him very often. And he didn't want to be called. To call out a smaller amount that he might be able to give, and in front of everyone? That was embarrassing.

Wally: That carried over heavily to me. That really carried over.

Toni: Oh, it was awful. Think about it now; it was horrific. To do that to people when it's a—when it's a community with so many refugees.

Wally: I remember there were others, like I'm sure you know, others who were snobs but who had very little money—they just made it even more difficult.

Toni: No compassion. My dislike for the practices in that synagogue affected me too. I didn't like those people, some of them made me feel uncomfortable. I wasn't friends with many of them, and I feel like nearly all of my friends then were relatives. They were my real friends, who I loved and trusted. But I had a small group of friends from synagogue—Mrs. Strauss for example. We're still friends to this day.

Wally: I always thought your tendency to congregate with relatives was a result of the Holocaust. That and being from a small village. Did that have an effect on you?

Toni: One of the last pieces of advice my mother gave me as we left Germany was to be careful in America. "Watch out for swindlers, don't trust those you don't know, keep close to the family," these words were always in my head. Perhaps I had a problem trusting outsiders.

Wally: Is that why you never joined any social clubs?

Toni: I never would have been part of something at the synagogue. The Sisterhood was not of interest of me, I didn't want to go there. But I kept busy taking care of all of my children.

Wally: Right.

Toni: I really could not go beyond that, and I did not want to.

Wally: Well, you had responsibilities.

Toni: But there was once an auction. That's how they raised money for the synagogue. The synagogue asked for volunteers to stand behind a booth and sell items. And I remember at the time I couldn't imagine that. That was not something I felt comfortable doing. I probably could have done it, perhaps well, but I didn't want to.

Wally: But you did go to the YMCA to learn English, right? So language wasn't a barrier. You actually learned English long before Dad ever did if I recall.

Toni: Your father learned English, it's just that he didn't use it very much. There was no opportunity. At the stockyards people did speak English, but the German immigrants spoke German to one another. Do you remember him speaking English when you were school age?

Wally: No. Well with his friends it was always German, but I think he spoke English sometimes—he definitely did later in his life. But it was rare when we first got here, even as he became better with English. I mean, I never expected you and Dad to come to school. If there was an assembly, sometimes parents would want to come to an assembly; I remember that other parents did. And it didn't bother me, but I clearly recall that you and Dad never attended. I remember it was different for Helen though.

Toni: She was born in the United States, so she wasn't an immigrant. She didn't see this country the same way as you and Herbert and Irene.

Wally: She once told me that she never did anything that would cause you and Dad to get called to school because what would the school do to you—in the sense of causing stress, communication issues, and expectations. It was ironic, I know she wanted you to come to the assemblies like other parents but at the same time, she wanted to protect you and keep you away from the "system".

Toni: Did you feel the same?

Wally: It was never an issue for me. I did my work, I was a top student, and there never was reason for you or Dad to come to school other than assemblies or graduation. You never had to go to my school in Germany, why would you go in Chicago?

Toni: But Helen was a very good student too.

Wally: Yes, and I was surprised to hear that her fear may have been part of her motivation. I think about it a lot when I look at my kids; there was a role reversal. Helen tried so hard to protect you and Dad, make it easy for you by staying out of trouble and getting good grades. She didn't want you to be involved for your own sake. Meanwhile with my kids, and I know Helen and Herb with their kids, are all such involved parents with our kids' schooling. We wanted to attend everything to the point our kids didn't want us there because we were embarrassing.

Toni: Why would it have been bad had I come to school?

Wally: It would be great to see you come to a school function, but what if one of us kids got a bad grade? The school would call you and then you would have to come in and talk to somebody about it. There was a worry of the language barrier and also explaining student expectations.

Toni: You may be correct. Your father and I couldn't help with your homework.

Wally: I always used to laugh because in high school they would give you instructions about how to do your homework. "Find a desk at home. Find a lamp that goes over your left shoulder so it doesn't hurt your eyes. Then sit there and work at your desk and have it quiet." And I'd think, what kind of—what world—where is that? Dick and Jane and Spot, you know? Who were they talking about? It had nothing to do with anybody we knew or the way we lived, at all. It just wasn't like that.

Toni: And to your father, school was not important to him. He thought if any of you got into trouble in school, quit school. He wanted to open that store with Herb, maybe even you. And Helen was a girl, and he didn't think that girls needed a good education in America.

Expectations were different. Women didn't need a good education, but still would work. I remember once saying to your father, "you wouldn't want me to go out and work, would you? You wouldn't want me to go out and work and get a job and I wouldn't be home for you and the children?" I was scared that I was going to have to go out and work in a store. I didn't want to imagine that. I wanted to be home, where I felt safest, to care for you and Helen and Irene.

Wally: And we didn't want you to go out and work. Part of it was protectionism, but it was also nice having you there, especially since Dad had to leave so early and come back so late. I know Helen really appreciated having you there. If you had gone to work, I'm sure you would have been very good at it.

Toni: Really, you think so?

Wally: Yea, absolutely. I think you would have been successful.

Toni: I thank you, that's quite flattering.

Wally: Well, at first I worried about what I perceived to be shyness, but as you've gotten older and I've seen you speak more at family events, you always do quite well. Now I don't see it as much as inherent shyness, but just a hesitation being in a new, foreign place which you've obviously overcome.

Toni: It was more than hesitation. I found myself scared stiff at times when we first arrived. It had to do with the strange relationship between all of the immigrant Jews here in Chicago. I always felt that the immigrant Jews from big cities looked down on me as a Jew from a small village. I didn't like that, and so I didn't like them. Maybe I came off as a snob, or shy… or even jealous.

Wally: They looked down on you even though everyone was a poor immigrant? Even though you had all that education back in Germany?

Toni: They came from big cities. They knew music. Opera. But over time I became friends with some of them. I became friends with people of whom I might have been jealous.

Wally: I never remember you saying anything bad about them. And I don't remember anybody ever saying anything bad about you.

Toni: I always tried to be nice. Honest, but nice. That was important to me. It also helped that as your father and I got older, we had more money.

Wally: You never spent much, plus we all got the German reparation money, which made a big difference.

Toni: What year did we start getting German money?

Wally: In 1953 I signed the papers in Marburg. In 1955 the payments started. I got $5,000 for education—so did Herb and Irene. All of the German refugee children got that.

Toni: And your father and I got reparations. I lived off that, still do. That and your father's social security. It saved me. Many people in the Selfhelp home—though not anymore—lived that way. They received social security and their reparations and it made it possible for them to live there.

Wally: So both you and Dad got reparations simultaneously?

Toni: Not at first. A husband and wife were given one joint payment. But when your father died, the reparation payments were transferred to me.

Wally: How much do you get monthly in reparations?

Toni: It's close to $1,000 a month. I'm surprised to hear you only got one payment of $5,000, I thought you received more. I also thought Helen was given an amount.

Wally: Helen never got anything since she wasn't born in Germany —even thought she was conceived there. But around the time I got my payment, Herb, Irene, Helen and I each got a small inheritance from Dad's brother, our Uncle Leopold.

Toni: Oh, it was from Leopold's wife, Alice. It was in Alice's will. Leopold died years earlier and left everything to her; they had no

children. Your father and Leopold were among nine children actually but only three or four others survived the Holocaust—they got
out of Germany before the Holocaust.

Wally: I remember Uncle Morris got out of Germany and escaped to
England, but I heard he died of a heart attack soon after he arrived.

Toni: Yes, in London. And your Uncle Jacob went to Israel—I never saw him again.

Wally: I saw him. I stayed with him when I spent a year in Israel in
1952–1953. He died during that year. He has a daughter Ilse a little
older than I who is still alive. How many years was it before Dad
and Uncle Leopold saw each other?

Toni: Your father saw him once. He never came to Chicago, your
father eventually went to New York. They'd also seen each other
the day we arrived on the boat in New York, but Leopold didn't put
us up. He and Alice greeted us and then went on their way. He had
the money to put us up but didn't. I didn't like him after that.

Wally: I always thought that they were just brothers—literally that's
all they were—two brothers. They didn't see each other or talk otherwise.

Toni: Your father couldn't go to see Leopold in New York during
the early years—there was no money. Leopold could have come
here though. Leopold never visited, but his wife Alice came to Chicago a few times and each time I made dinner. And Alice once said
"oh, this dinner is so delicious—so much better than last time." I
always thought she had nothing but contempt for us until you graduated law school.

Wally: Oh, when I finished law school at the University of Chicago,
Leopold tried to entice me to come to New York. He wanted Herb
to come to New York first but Herb already had a job. So Leopold

then wanted me to work for him, selling men's clothing

Toni: Leopold died before your father; he died in 1962. That was one of the times that Alice came to visit. She also came when a cousin's nephew had his bar mitzvah. Do you remember that? She didn't actually come for the bar mitzvah, it's just that it happened at that time. Didn't she stay with you and your family?

Wally: Yes, she stayed with us. She loved tennis.. She took me to the Forest Hills tennis matches—you know, the US Open. That was when she served on boards and also played tennis. She could not understand how I could go to Israel after finishing college and law school. She just didn't understand.

Toni: I think Alice was in the arts at the time. She definitely didn't like peasant Jews.

Wally: I don't remember her and her manners bothering Dad much.

Toni: I think you're right—and if it was an issue he never admitted it. But, yes, Alice was just another big city person who looked down on me for being from a village. But I didn't attend the traditional school system and didn't know about all of these fancy things. I hated that. You know, Alice died when her nephew stabbed her. She was at dinner party with him and she insulted him. I can't imagine what she said, but he stabbed her in someone's home.

Wally: I had forgotten about that. Just terrible.

Toni: A bitter end. But your father; what bothered him was not others looking down us for being village Jews. Instead it was money; that we didn't have enough.

MARKUS' LATER YEARS

I want to speak a little more about Dad and his relationships with his children. When I remember Dad, I remember him from Germany where he was successful and everyone liked him. I saw some of that later on—when he got social, when he was friendly, when he was kidding around with people in the States. But there was so much less of that in Chicago, especially in Helen's eyes. Based on her stories of Dad when she was growing up, after Herb and I were off at college or had jobs, she remembers him so differently; not at all in the way I remember him. But I only lived at home for about eight years when we arrived in Chicago before starting college, and for some of it I was working or in school—so I spent little time there, and that's probably why I pictured Dad as he was in Germany. It was more of a shock for me to see Dad in the later years. While Helen remembers him being reserved and less friendly overall, I saw him going from being a capable, well liked guy to being depressed in those last years. That reserve that Helen saw as part of his nature, I saw as a product of his depression.

My cousin Otto tells a story about my father's kindness. One time when Otto was a young boy back in Roth, he threw a chicken into an outhouse toilet. This caused a great deal of consternation to people. Markus stepped in and got the chicken out, saving Otto from getting into deep water from his family. Markus didn't tell who had caused this disturbance.

Toni: In Chicago in his later years I recall he would have one day that he was okay and the following day he would talk about going out and harming himself. And I would stand at the door, pulling him away from it.

Wally: I remember on the good days Dad really used to love to flirt with Helen's friends. It was that charm that he showed all the time in Germany which I knew he had, and yet Helen almost seemed taken aback by it—not in a bad way—she was just surprised.

Toni: Oh yes, he did flirt with all of Helen's little friends… and as I recall, you did too, Wally. But your father liked it and I liked it too. I was just as surprised as Helen to see this friendliness come out in him. It reminded me of our time in Germany.

Wally: In Germany he was a very, very well liked person. When I returned for a visit in 1953, the first thing I heard from our old neighbors was, "when is Markus coming? When is Markus coming back?"

Toni: That's so sad. That was around the time his health really started declining. Helen and Irene were still living at home, but you were in Israel and Herb was working.

Wally: Yes, I remember you wrote me in Israel that Dad was sick and I arranged to return home. And he was a little better by the time I got home, though not in good health by any means. It was that way for a few years after.

Toni: It was in 1958, about three or four years later that he had his first electric shock therapy.

Wally: Well at first I thought he was just depressed.

Toni: But he had become sick in the stockyards. He worked in a cold chamber—as a boner, cutting the animals and the meat off the bone—for how many years?

Wally: Twenty years at least.

Toni: And it was hard. He got very sick right before the first shock treatment. He had a blood clot in his leg and they thought he would die.

Wally: I remember they called from the hospital.

Toni: I refused to go. They needed somebody to go to the hospital. They told me about how they needed to operate on his leg or he would die.

Wally: The clot had to be removed and they, the hospital, needed somebody to sign. So I went to the hospital. First the doctor explained it to me and then I signed the forms. At that time it was a very, very difficult surgery to perform.

Toni: And he survived it.

Wally: A successful operation; he came out of that.

Toni: But that was the first of a lot of problems to come.

Wally: How often did he threaten to harm himself?

Toni: I always felt it was just talk.

Wally: How was he was he after the electric shock treatment?

Toni: It was successful in 1958. Well, success is…

Wally: Relative. But he was happier, stopped talking about harming himself?

Toni: They didn't speak of giving him shock treatment again until the early '60s.

Wally: Who was his doctor? You remember his name?

Toni: I don't remember. It was a horrible man.

Wally: Lousy guy.

Toni: I remember one doctor who came to the house when your father was ill. He had collapsed—he had some kind of weakness. We called, and by this time it was the early 60's and your father and I were living on Kingston Avenue in South Shore. It was Saturday morning… it was so awful. The doctor made some comment about how your father is old.

Wally: He had atrial fibrillation; enlarged heart, high blood pressure—all those things.

Toni: And another ailment. With the "a".

Wally: Arteriosclerosis.

Toni: I started having a vision. I didn't want to answer the home phone when your father was out. I feared the next call was going to be about him; that something had happened.

Wally: But Dad got better when a new grandchild was born—my son Ari. It was 1961.

Toni: Oh, that was the happiest thing for him. He was very, very excited.

Wally: Very excited about it. He was always ready to take the baby for a walk in the carriage. He would take Ari in the buggy and push him over to the fire station.

Toni: I have a couple of these pictures that are wonderful.

Toni: Right. I remember that Ari would get excited when your father took the buggy and followed the garbage truck. Ari wanted to be a garbage man.

Wally: Ari loved anything that moved. The trains, buses, trucks. And Dad obliged, pushing that buggy so Ari had a good view of it all.

Toni: Your father thought it was wonderful. And I of course, thought it was nice too.

Wally: And then one day, something happened. Ari ran—he was sort of a wild kid—ran in the park and fell and skinned his knee. And he came home bleeding.

Toni: Your father was hysterical.

Wally: Dad was very upset. But Ari was a little kid—it was going to happen, for goodness sake. However, Dad was blamed.

Toni: So, he blamed himself.

Wally: No, he was blamed.

Toni: By whom?

Wally: All of the women in the family.

Toni: I don't recall, but if I did it was for Ari's safety.

Wally: And after that he didn't take Ari out anymore.

Toni: Anymore at all? I remember going out with your father and Ari when Ari could walk.

Wally: Well, alone. Dad wasn't allowed to take Ari out alone.

Toni: This was all around 1964, correct?

Wally: Yes. You know, Ari fell down the back stairs of our house once—but Dad was not there, thank goodness for that. Another time Ari returned home bleeding on the back of his head. Come to think of it, Ari got himself hurt a lot, but only once was it blamed on someone else. When Dad was older, he came over frequently to my new home at 6840 S. Euclid in the Jackson Park Highlands. He came over to help us weed and plant, which he liked very much. I think it reminded him of his home in Germany. He loved it, but one day he pulled out some flowers by mistake.

Toni: Oh, no.

Wally: That was trouble. I was none too pleased myself. But it can happen. He had deteriorated at that point. It was 1966 or so, soon before he died.

Toni: And I couldn't help him anymore. He became very depressed. The doctors suggested we take him to Michael Reese Hospital's psychiatric ward. Which I believe was a mistake, but I was scared.

Wally: Why were you scared? Because he was so depressed?

Toni: Yes, I was scared that something might happen to him. Helen worried that he might hurt himself. He'd say something and I'd say "don't say that." I wouldn't have known what to do if he got sick or if he, by some chance, actually had hurt himself.

Wally: I remember visiting him frequently at Michael Reese Hospital with Chaya. The first time we went there we were mildly shocked because he was put in a locked ward. But whenever we were there we would reassure him. I made a point to talk about the future. One of the things I remember saying to him was "Dad, you want to keep positive, stay healthy. You want to be here for Ari's bar mitzvah." Anyway a couple days after that conversation, I got a call at my office. Helen called me. The hospital had called her at home. She didn't want to be the one to call you.

Toni: Called and said what?

Wally: That Dad was dead.

Toni: Oh, no. She didn't want to tell me?

Wally: He drowned early in the morning in the bathtub.

Toni: And they said he committed suicide.

Wally: Right, that's what the doctor in the ward said.

Toni: That's what I thought. They had said he slit his wrists.

Wally: That's exactly right—that's what they said.

Toni: I hadn't gone to the hospital the night before. I hadn't seen your father for two days.

Wally: Since Helen didn't want to tell you alone, we went to your apartment together. By the time we got there, representatives from the hospital were there already there to deliver the news. I will always remember coming down the block—I could hear you shrieking.

Toni: I don't even remember.

Wally: I could hear it out the windows, down the street. I had to go identify the body and so I went to Michael Reese Hospital. I was very upset about it. I got there within an hour. They'd already moved the body. So then I had to go to the coroner's office. I talked to the doctor at the hospital first. He had some story about how Dad had committed suicide. I said "how is it possible that this happened?"

Toni: Right. In a closed ward they are supposed to watch people.

Wally: Yeah, the doctor said something about a bath.

I asked, "And don't you have somebody watching people?"

And he didn't answer.

I said, "How did he drown?"

He drowned – he must – he um – he must have slit his wrists.

"Why is the body not here?"

Why is – well, we...

He was very, very evasive. He knew I was a lawyer.

Toni: Of course.

Wally: So, I did go to the coroner; I saw Dad's body. I asked to see his slit wrists. When I told the coroner he looked at me with an awkward expression. He said if there was a slit on Dad's wrists, it wasn't evident. "Your father died by drowning; there wouldn't be any wounds." I told him not to worry about it. I went to his desk and picked up the death certificate. The certificate says death by drowning. And so I happen to think that Dad didn't kill himself. I think he drowned. Whatever happened, maybe he had a heart attack in the bathtub, maybe whatever, you know? But regardless the hospital was terribly negligent. The doctors in the ward did everything they could to ignore me; they obviously didn't want to talk about it. Maybe they should have been sued. In fact I called one of lawyers in litigation at my office and we talked about the legal implications. My partner said, "what's the point of it—are you going to fight this?" He advised against litigation. It wasn't worth it.

Toni: I agreed with you.

Wally: There was nothing to be done afterwards.

Toni: I cannot imagine profiting from your father's death.

Wally: That's why I made that decision.

Toni: I'm glad we agree that your father never would have been the type of man to take his own life.

Wally: I just don't think it was in his nature.

Toni: Why was he by himself in a bathtub? It was so awful.

Wally: And also, Dad hadn't done anything to himself before.

Toni: No, he hadn't done anything, but he talked about it. He did talk about it.

Wally: Well I guess we still don't know exactly what happened that day. Regardless, he died a tragic death in a locked psychiatric ward. I am sure that his death most certainly was the result of everything that happened to him and his family as a result of the Nazi disaster.

Toni: No matter what we all miss him terribly.

Wally: Helen and I talked about Dad once she knew more about the actual story of leaving Germany. I think the word she used to describe what happened to you and Dad was "deformed." She felt like both of your lives were taken away, and I can agree with that.

Toni: That must have been years later, I didn't talk about leaving Germany much after we got America; with her or with anyone. Your father never spoke of it.

Wally: Really, neither did I. I rarely talked about it with my children until they were grown up.

Toni: Your poor father. It was tough enough to come here from Germany, and go through the experience. Of course, we all survived but nothing can prepare you for the death of your family, and he suffered. It was hard for me too, for many of the people in our neighborhood in Chicago. I say there is nothing about the hardships of his life, your father's life, that wasn't heartbreaking.

Wally: Yes. Absolutely.

Toni: I never believed he committed suicide. Knowing about the drowning now, I believe that even more. I still, though, feel guilty for putting him in the hospital.

Wally: You cannot blame yourself. It was all of our decision.

Toni: But suddenly he's by himself…in a locked room.

*   *   *

*[Wally: **What made life so difficult** for my father when he came to Chicago? After all he was a relatively young man. He had served with honor in the German army for four years during the First World War. He had received several medals. He was married to a beautiful young women and had established himself as a well respected citizen, owner of a large house and some land. But after the Nazis arose to power in 1933, the lack of a formal education in university, which was available in Marburg, would come to haunt him. By June 1938 when he was fortunate enough to escape with his family to Chicago, he would find himself as a refugee without any assets—tangible or intangible—that would enable him to live a life which would give him some feelings of satisfaction and status in his new community. Perhaps this is the definition of a refugee. I don't know. Perhaps some refugees, because of their background and assets can adjust more quickly to gain a new basis for their existence but my father could not. Except for his wife there was no one he*

could look to for assistance. Instead he had young children to worry about. In addition, he was a *dorf Jude*, a Jew from a small village who had low social status in the German immigrant society in Chicago. Further he did not participate in social or sports clubs. His own synagogue was not a particularly warm place for him because of his poverty, and the only work he could find was considered low in status, especially among the Jewish community. Then within a few years of his arrival he learned that much of his family had been killed by the Nazis. Within 15 years after his arrival he became seriously ill. This obviously had a terrible effect on his state of mind.]

IRENE

While the escape to America saved our lives, the move was particularly difficult for Irene. The mental problems with which she was
born made the transition challenging in many ways. She was not
given the kind of help a child like her would receive now. Thus she
was exposed to many hardships. But we worked with the doctors.
We did what we could based on the information at the time.

Toni: You were born in 1929; Irene was born in 1924.

Wally: She was five years older than me, but a few times during our
schooling we were put in the same grade, which was not an easy
thing for us. I started in kindergarten at Kenwood (which was an
elementary school at the time) and then jumped to third grade at
Ray School and progressed at my age level. Irene did not progress
at the same rate, so I would sometimes be in her class. Later on it
was okay. Nobody ever said anything against her. I saw it whenever
I was in her grade. She had this one girl who was a friend. They
lived at the end of our block on Kenwood. Irene didn't have many
other friends. Anyway, when you look at the middle school grade
picture, you'll see Irene and me in the same class.

Toni: For how long was that? Not very long.

Wally: No, she graduated from there and she went to the Wilson High School [a trade school on the North Side].

Toni: Your father brought her there. She went there for a year or two.

Wally: He took her there at first, but that couldn't last. She had to go by herself. And I couldn't go with her, I was too young. They let her graduate middle school a year before me, but she should have been finishing high school at that time. I think about the whole thing with Irene, I remember how much I cared for her, but how difficult she could be. And she caused friction in the family. Helen once compared her to the Brothers Karamazov—you know, how there's one person who set off the whole family.

Toni: I know Irene meant so much to your father, but it was hard for him. She had special needs. And I think it became harder after Selma died. I don't remember her birth in Germany. I was not there when Selma gave birth.

Wally: I talked to our cousin Elfrieda about it later I learned that Irene was born prematurely. That's one thing. I heard that when Irene was born, they kept her in a little shoebox. That's how I know she was premature. It may have been at birth that there was a problem that caused brain damage. I have tried to put in perspective what Irene went through. It is so ridiculous to talk about with sixty years of hindsight because I feel guilty, just like Dad and the psychiatric ward.

Toni: Well, there was something about Irene. When you were little, when Helen was little, you both played with Irene. As soon as you both got old enough to realize that there was something different about her, you and Helen stopped playing with her as much. I also saw it with one of our cousins who was younger than Helen. As soon as she realized that there was something wrong, the playing stopped. It happened repeatedly—a person would see Irene's disability and stop coming—it was an awful treatment of Irene.

Wally: None of us knew what to do. Even later on when we knew what to do, we didn't have the wherewithal and it was really hard.

Toni: For her it must have been very bad. I didn't know what do with her. Your father would get so angry with Irene. I remember how worried he became over Irene's citizenship exam. Do you remember that?

Wally: I remember there was this terror in the house that she wasn't going to pass her citizenship exams.

Toni: I was scared.

Wally: The stress probably took years off of Dad's life.

Toni: Everyone was trying to teach her things. She had so much to memorize, and we were all worried.

Wally: But she did pass. It was about five years after we got to Chicago.

Toni: So 1944 or 1945. It was so hard. We had to care for her on our own. At that time there was nothing. No social programs—or none that I knew of—that we could enroll in or participate in. At first we did not understand her problems. Except we knew that she was stubborn and she wouldn't do what your father told her.

Wally: That's right. I remember this. She would refuse to eat beans. I remember beans. And I remember once hollering at her for that, yelling at her. I was a little boy back in Roth—six or seven years old. My father yelled at me for yelling at her, saying that he was the boss in the house, not me.

Toni: When she was already grown, Irene had this obsession. She loved True Story magazine. It was full of fictional stories like serials—a soap opera in a magazine. The magazines were seven or ten pages long. Irene would hide them in her drawers and under her bed.

Wally: Helen told me that whenever you found them in Irene's room you would throw them away; thought the magazines were bad for Irene.

Toni: They were junk, just like TV these days.

Wally: Well looking back at it now, I think it was great that she was reading.

Toni: It was bad literature. I wished Irene would go to a library, but she didn't do that.

Wally: That's what I think about as I get older—we sort of worked at destroying whatever enjoyment Irene had. We went after it and really—I didn't feel bad back then. If anything, I thought I just thought I have this *crazy* sister. It was terrible, but...

Toni: There was no understanding then.

Wally: We had no control—she'd go, get out of the house and do her own thing.

Toni: Well our other option was to put her in an institution. But that never happened. We never looked for it.

Wally: We never considered it. I remember at one point, the first time Irene was hospitalized, we'd gone to see her. Afterwards, Helen and Herb and I were outside of the hospital's billing department, talking about it. And Helen said, "Well, you know, we really should think of finding someplace for her to go."

Toni: I think the first time maybe Irene took pills, that was something that made us notice. She was in the hospital. When was this?

Wally: Well it was after I was married already to Chaya. I'd say the early '60s, well before Dad died. And anyway, Helen made this suggestion, and Herb and I acted as though she was suggesting exiling Irene or something like that. Helen obviously wasn't even sure of the idea herself so she immediately dropped it.

Toni: So, how did the conversation end? What happened?

Wally: Nothing. I mean, we all saw placing her somewhere as institutionalization and something bad because we didn't know from anything. And this is a family, who by that time, were pretty educated. And yet we really acted very uneducated. I don't think Irene ever talked about the first hospitalization, did she?

Toni: No, no, no. I think things became desperate for her after your father died. And I never realized how close she was emotionally to him, even though they fought a great deal.

Wally: I think for Dad, Irene was like this person who reminded him of every bad thing that he'd ever confronted. You know, Selma's death, Germany, his job, everything.

Toni: Perhaps.

Wally: Was Irene working at the Selfhelp home at the time?

Toni: No, she was working at a stationary store.

Wally: And getting along pretty well if I recall. She went by herself. She had to take a train.

Toni: And one morning the shop called. Her employer said that she had not arrived. He asked, "where was she?" I said she left home hours ago.

Wally: I remember the employer called you and you called me. I left my office and headed to your apartment.

Toni: When you arrived at the house, we ran straight to the lake but we didn't find her.

Wally: I remember we went home and called the police. They sent a helicopter over. I know about the helicopter because one of our relatives lived up on Lake Shore Drive. They saw the helicopter. But the police didn't find her. But someone found her shoes on the beach.

Toni: Helen came home and stayed with me after you left for the office because something was very wrong. Later I got a phone call from the police.

Wally: Then I got a phone call.... Irene been found on the beach by the Coast Guard.

Toni: Helen and Chaya went down to the beach—I stayed home. Helen identified the body there because I didn't want to.

Wally: And I went to the coroner's office to identify her body and do the paperwork.

Toni: She had tried to commit suicide before that, though. There was a time when she took pills.

Wally: That's right.

Toni: And maybe that's when she went to the hospital. It's possible. She had a psychiatrist for a time. And when she committed suicide she was seeing a psychiatrist.

Wally: But there'd been an enormous amount of deterioration in the last year of her life. Helen told me that Irene thought Mike Royko of the Chicago Tribune was writing about her in the paper.

Toni: It was hard. It was just me and Irene in the apartment after your father died. But you know what I remember about it most?

What I remember about that, Wally, is I remember being so grateful to you. The cops were calling. The Tribune called the house and wanted a story about the suicide and I remember you talked to them. You said to them, "this is not a story."

Wally: Correct.

Toni: The rest of us did not know what to say. I could not talk to the news. And there was too much with everything else... the problems in the cemetery. That was an issue.

Wally: Well, theoretically, you're not supposed to bury a person who commits suicide in a Jewish cemetery.

Toni: That's right.

Wally: But we buried her in Chevra-Kadisha Cemetery. I just told them I knew the man that ran the cemetery. I was one of the cemetery's attorneys. So we buried her. Unrelated, I had the same type of problem years later with somebody who wasn't circumcised. So their cemetery president calls me and says "What are you going to do? He's not circumcised." So I said, "Well, circumcise him." And that's what they did.

*   *   *

[Wally: After Irene's death I had some deep soul searching on the tragedies that occurred in our family and wondered whether there was something I could have done personally. I remembered that when I met my Uncle Leopold in New York (on my way to Israel) he offered me a job, in his business selling fine materials (linens, suits, and the like), which I refused. I told him I had finished law school at the University of Chicago. It almost seemed as though he was my father (he had no children) and said I owed it to him to work for him.

This reminded me of my own father who, while he never said anything to me directly, I knew he did not approve of my decision to go to law school. And he didn't seem happy about my going to Israel. Even though as I recall it I assured him that I would be coming back from Israel. When I departed early in the morning I went out to the corner to be picked up for a ride to the train to New York for the ship to Israel. My father appeared on his way to his work at the stockyards with tears in his eyes. We hugged and he left for work.

In New York I boarded an Italian ship carrying many Jewish passengers on their way to Israel. I was assigned my own cabin, with the fare being paid by a Jewish organization. I was headed for Israel to work for Sherut L'Am as a volunteer, working half a day in Kibbutz Ma'aleh Hahamisha and studying the other half of the day, with a minimum commitment of one year. It was a marvelous year with wonderful experiences, teachers, and *tiyulim* (tours, trips within Israel). It was *tsena* (a period of scarcity in Israel)—everything was scarce but spirits were high. To this day I have a high degree of affection for the kibbutz.

I received many letters from Toni as well as packages containing chocolate and other goodies.

I had relatives and friends in Israel. By the summer of 1953 I was faced with the decision of whether to stay in Israel or return home. There were people who were willing to assist me if I stayed. The kibbutz offered me an opportunity to go to a training course to become a kibbutz lawyer. I also met with Shimon Agranat, a judge of the Israeli Supreme Court. Someone from the kibbutz knew him. Agranat, a fellow graduate of the University of Chicago Law School, offered to assist me in becoming a lawyer in Israel. He was rather optimistic about my future if I remained in Israel.

But then I received a letter from Toni, telling me that my father was ill—that he had heart problems, is my recollection now. This letter made my decision easy—I decided to return to Chicago to see what was going on with my father. I returned to Chicago in September of 1953.

I was almost penniless but I had enough for my ticket. I boarded a ship in Haifa bound for Cannes, France. There I slept on the beach for two nights, to save my last dollars, and then boarded my ship for New York. I came to New York where my brother and his wife picked me up at a visitors' station outside the city. They had been on vacation in New England and Toni arranged for them to meet me. Except they were two days late.

My father was ill when I arrive home. Apparently he had collapsed and was now recovering. He went back to work in the stockyards. But this was the beginning stage of a long series of illnesses. He later developed a serious blood clot that had to be operated on.

My return from Israel was of course timely and I have no regrets about missed opportunities. My deepest regrets—or feelings of guilt—were that I was not able to be of more assistance to my father. His greatest wish was to operate a business with his son, in which he could work for himself as he had in Germany. In Germany he farmed land we owned. He grew vegetables and fruit trees. He also operated a business supplying seed grain to farmers and had a small store in Niederwalgern.

While feeling guilty over not being able to help my father in this manner, I know that in the end my father was able to see me take advantage of opportunities in my career as a lawyer. Dean Edward Levi of the Law School told me that I had a good shot at becoming a clerk for a federal judge because of my top record in law school. Ordinarily I might have been able to try for a Supreme Court clerkship, but McCarthyism made that difficult for University of Chicago graduates in those years. So Dean Levi arranged an interview for me with Judge Luther M. Swygert, who had been appointed by FDR as a federal judge for the Northern District of Indiana. It was a wonderful opportunity for me to work under a fine judge. Judge Swygert became a supporter of Israel and visited many times. I like to think I had something to do with that.]

TONI'S LATER YEARS

After Irene died, Toni lived alone for a few years and then chose to move into the Selfhelp Home, where she ended up living for nearly 25 years. She lived an independent life, in a place where she was nearly self-reliant, and was able to entertain and receive her grandchildren easily. Chaya and I wanted Toni to move in with us but she refused. She insisted that it would be better for us and for her if she moved to the Selfhelp Home.

The Selfhelp Home is a retirement home established in Chicago in the 1930s by German Jewish immigrants, first in Hyde Park and later in Uptown. Nearly all the residents were German Jewish refugees with similar backgrounds and some common experiences. Some were related to each other or were close friends from back home in Germany. This was true not only of the residents, but of the many German Jews who were involved in the administration of Selfhelp. Dorothy Becker, who was the manager of the Selfhelp at the time Toni moved in, was also a German Jewish refugee. She is the one who hired me and my law firm D'Ancona Pflaum Wyatt & Riskind to do legal work for the home and also for residents of the home, in the areas of estate planning and probate. I have many memories of those years, particularly relating to refugees who had problems relating to the loss of family members and property in

Germany. There was an almost family kind of atmosphere at the Selfhelp Home. Residents had their meals in a common dining room—my wife and I often joined Toni for Shabbat meals and for Jewish holidays. Even by the time Toni moved there in the 1970s the food was often from German recipes familiar to the refugees and survivors who were moving to the Selfhelp Home in their older years. Toni felt at home there. Towards the end of her life Toni had a caretaker named Rose, who was from the Philippines. Toni always had cookies on hand for Rose and other staff members. Toni's very last words to her caretaker were to try some soup she had liked. To this day we are still in contact with Rose.

I made a number of trips to Roth, Germany with my family over the years, but Toni and Markus always refused to visit Germany, even when invited by German authorities. Toni lived until she was 99 ½ years of age. Her funeral services were at Congregation Rodfei Zedek in Chicago. Rabbi Gertel gave the eulogy. I felt that it was a moving and thoughtful presentation of her life. Toni was buried at Chevra Kadisha alongside Markus.

EULOGY FOR TONI STERN ROTH

by Rabbi Elliot B. Gertel, January 30, 1998

Toni Stern was, to her family and friends, a beacon of warmth, love and concern who left them beaming with joy, self-confidence and moral upliftment every time they were privileged to see her.

Her life began almost a century ago in the village of Roth in Germany. Her father, Mannes, ran a dry goods store with his brothers. Her mother, Bertha, helped out with the business and presided over a joyous home, dedicated to the Jewish faith and its moral teachings. Toni was devoted to her parents and to her brothers Louis and Hugo, to her uncles and their families, and to her childhood town, where many of the Jewish families were related. She helped out in her family's store, beginning as a child. As a young woman she delivered merchandise on her bicycle to other villages. She attended school in her small community's two room schoolhouse, and then attended trade school in the nearby town of Giessen. She then returned home to work hard in the family business for several years.

In 1936, when she was 38 years old, she married Markus Roth, a widower, whose wife Selma had been a cousin of Toni's. Selma passed away at the age of 34, leaving two sons, Herbert and Walter, and a daughter, Irene. There was never a moment's doubt in Toni's mind that she could and would become a good mother to these children. She was devoted to Markus and to the children, and couple of years later she and Markus were blessed with a daughter Helen, who was born in Chicago. In Germany, Markus' family was in the flour and fertilizer business, and they farmed a bit as well, growing potatoes and other vegetables.

Getting to Chicago was no easy matter. Toni could see the day by day horrors occurring in her country of Germany, and in her small town. Friends and neighbors were turning on the small Jewish community, hinting openly that soon there would be no Jewish community. It was through Toni's relatives, the Rosenbusch family of Kokomo, Indiana, that Markus, Toni and the children were able to get affidavits. Toni's mother and brothers could not get affidavits in time, and perished in the Holocaust. They urged her to leave, but it was, of course, excruciating for her to leave them.

As it happens, we are reading in the Torah of the plague of darkness that came over Egypt. Our sages teach that the darkness, which came because of the blind hatred that leads one people to enslave another, was palpable. It had substance. You could feel it. It was a lot like the darkness that Germany had made for itself. Yet the Torah says, "All the children of Israel had light in their dwellings."

Toni's family believes that the light she brought into their lives and into the world for over fifty years after her terrible loss of family and friends, after her world was turned upside down, was due to the light and love and morality in her family and in the small Jewish community of Roth, due to the spirit of cooperation and mutual support found not only in Toni's parents' home but in the family store, which united her with uncles and cousins, and in the synagogue and mikvah supported by her small rural Jewish community. Her family believes that she found her strength in that family and community heritage, and in her devotion to the traditions and teachings Judaism. Her strong and abiding sense of right and wrong, inculcated in her by her parents, by the example of their own integrity in business and the home, ever guided her.

Life was not easy for Toni in Chicago. Markus worked hard as a butcher, from 5 am to 5 pm, at a packing house in the stockyards. He came home exhausted, yet always had his spirits boosted by Toni's devotion. She had to take in boarders, into a home already filled with six people. Some people would come just for meals. She earned money for the household in this manner with charm, style and humor. She managed to find times to go to nearby playground with the children, taking them to the Point and to the movies. She found support and strength in her neighbors in South Shore, the Sterns, members of her extended family from Germany. She also found strength in her belief in America, especially in the Roosevelt-Democrat approach to American politics, which she constantly and eloquently defended throughout the years.

Toni was not content just to make do, but with verve and courage she undertook to get education and to do what she had to do creatively. She was one of the first on the block to take lessons in English. She immediately enrolled in a course at the YWCA. And if she was going to cook for boarders, she was going to be the best cook there was. After all, she was cooking for her family too. In her circles in South Shore, her white challah, bread, and cakes became legendary, especially to her family. In tribute to the love she put into her cooking as much as to her time cooking and baking, her family published a collection of her recipes, which gave her much nachas.

We are told that in the Temple of old there were special cakes called *levivot* from the word *lev* or heart, baked to show one's love of God and of fellow human beings. Toni always put great love into her cooking and baking. And she lavished that love upon her family. She delighted in her children-in-law Elsa, Chaya, and Lowell, whom she regarded as her children. She adored each and every grandchild and their spouses: Mark; Janet and Tony; Debbie and Jeff; Ari and Kate; Judy and Steve; Miriam and Mark. When the grandchildren were young, she would sing German and English songs to them to make them feel special. She learned about basketball and baseball in order to communicate with her grandchildren, and became an avid Bulls and Cubs fan in her own right. She always cautioned her children and grandchildren to be streetwise and to take care of themselves.

Whenever they visited, she would want them to eat something, to taste her love, and then lavish praise upon them, meaning every word, to nurture their self-esteem as she would nurture them with food and delight them with her baking. All the generations in her family understood that one had to eat something while visiting her.

When she could no longer bake herself, she bought the best cookies for her guests, particularly her favorite energy foods, which gave
her close to a century of life—so who can question her recipe—
were soup and cookies. She always had cookies on hand, as well,
for the staff of the Selfhelp home and for her devoted caregivers
who stayed with her in the daytime, Rose and Laurie. Toni's very
last words to Rose were to try some soup she had tasted and liked
at the Selfhelp home. She spoke constantly of her children and
grandchildren, and was proud of their character and achievements.
She was already praising their achievements and offering cookies to
the apples of her eye, her ten great grandchildren Daniel, Rachel,
Jessica, Evan, Leah, Isabel, Sophie, Miko, Jonah and Emma.

[Two great-granddaughters, Talia and Tema, and a great-great
granddaughter, Tuva, have been born since Toni's death.]

Whoever was privileged to enter Toni's home, whether in
South Shore or at the Selfhelp home, understood that behind the
baking and the cooking and the soup was a spiritual heritage that
guided her life and helped her to adjust to life in America and to
move beyond the darkness in her native Germany. In her cooking,
her humor, her principles, her character, just by listening to her
voice, her laugh, or looking into her eyes, one sensed the light that
the Children of Israel have or can have in their dwellings.

The Sabbath was important to her. She attended synagogue services every week. She used and knew the old Women's Prayer
Book she had brought from Germany, along with books about
Jewish history. She prayed with *kavanah*, with inwardness. She
walked all the way from South Shore to attend Ari's bar mitzvah.
Her own children remember that the Sabbath would be awaited
with the baking of challah and the scrubbing of the floors and their
being covered with newspapers, lest the Sabbath Bride arrive and
find anything soiled. For many years, Toni imparted the meaning
and teachings of all the Festivals of Israel to her family with her
cooking and baking and, above all, her devotion to God and her
graciousness and courtesy to people. She would never hurt or em-
barrass others.

It is told of one of the great Rabbis of the Talmud that whenever his mother approached, he would call out upon hearing her
footsteps: "I stand before the extension of God's presence." All
agree that Toni Stern Roth embodied the high ideals of Jewish
motherhood—the high standards, the giving nature, the constant
love and support, that we seek in our dear ones and in God. May
she rest in peace. May her memory ever be a blessing, even as we
affirm in our faith a life beyond this earthly life, in the Presence of
God. Of her we can say what Scripture says of the Woman of Val-
or:

Place before her the work of her hands, wherever people gath-
er her deeds speak her praise.

SWEET TRANSMISSION: THE RECIPES

Not only was Toni a "Woman of Valor," she was also a woman of many skills, among the chief of which were baking skills. These were undoubtedly a part of the heritage she received from her family through the generations.

We have been fortunate enough to obtain copies of written recipes produced by Toni's mother Berta, who undoubtedly had received these recipes from her own mother. Copies of Berta's recipes were found in her old house in Roth by the people who now live in the house, many years after Berta and her sons Louis and Hugo were deported by the Nazis. In 2011 these new owners were remodeling the house, when they found the packet of recipe. I include a picture of this packet which was sent to me by Gabi Schmidt, an active member of the Arbeitskreis, a German organization which was a prime mover in the restoration of the synagogue in Roth. The Arbeitskreis is actively engaged in education and research on the history of the Jews in Roth.

Toni brought her heritage of recipes with her to Chicago. Once in Chicago Toni wrote her own recipe notebook, some in German, some in English, and some in a mixture of the two. Below I include photos of some of the pages of Toni's recipe notebook.

A fourth generation member of Berta's family has added an-

Packet of recipes as found in 2011, in the former home
of Berta Stern in Roth, Germany.

other link to this tradition. In 1982 Toni's granddaughter, Deborah Roth-Howe (Herb's daughter) sat down with Toni and captured these recipes for transmission to a new generation. She created a cookbook called *The Best of Grandma Toni (and significant others)*.

One of the recipes in Toni's and Bertha's repertoire was a recipe for a chocolate cake. As a young child in Germany I recall helping Toni make the cake, by grating the chocolate for example. Once we were in Chicago I often assisted as well, chiefly by eating it on many occasions. I recall that when I graduated from Hyde Park High School in 1946 I went with some friends to study and work at a Zionist summer camp near the Berkshires. My only food during the daylong trip to the camp by bus from Chicago was a chocolate cake that my mother had baked for me and my friends. It turns out that the sweet taste of cookies and cakes is almost a basic tie that connects me to my parents and their ancestors and our common heritage. Toni's notebook from Chicago and the packet found in her mother's old house in Roth are both happy and sorrowful memories of the past.

* * *

I. Translations from German of some of the recipes from the packet found in Berta's old house.

Chocolate cake

Mix ¼ lb Tomor [a brand of margarine] with 200 gr. sugar, 300 gr. flour, ½ glass water, ¼ lb grated chocolate or 1 ½ spoonfuls of cocoa, 4 egg yolks, a pinch of cinnamon, a little baking soda, as much cloves. Mix again with a package of baking powder and then with 4 beaten egg whites to bake in a properly prepared baking pan.

If you want to make a chocolate frosting, take some chocolate, a little butter, and add a little water. Let it cook until it gets thick. Frosting should be put on the cake while still warm.

Matza meal cake

½ lb potato flour or one can also use matzo meal. Then take ½ lb sugar and 10 egg yolks mixed very well into the meal. Add a little water and let stand ¾ hour. Beat the egg whites to a snow [till stiff]. Fold in and bake.

Matzekrimsel

5 matzos, 3 egg yolks, 150 g sugar juice and zest of 1 lemon, some Sultanas [golden raisins], 1 pinch of salt, cinnamon, 3 egg whites. Soak the matzo, mix the egg yolks and sugar until frothy Add the remaining ingredients and the soaked matzo including the egg whites. Scoop out fritters and cook in fat.

Potato pancakes [prepared] in waffle iron

1 ½ kilo raw potatoes, grated and mixed with an egg, a spoonful of flour, 1/8 liter milk, salt, and a knifeful of baking soda. Then after the dough is mixed, spread fat in the waffle iron and bake until brown.

Bercheskloesse (challah dumplings)

Berches [a German-Jewish challah, the dough of which is made without eggs, but with a potato] soaked in fat, with the excess squeezed out, add salt, nutmeg, 3 eggs, knead properly, and cook in water.

II. Recipes from Toni's Chicago notebook, translated by my brother–in–law Lowell Dittmer.

Lemon Soup

8 glasses of water, 1 glass of sugar, ½ lemon peel, ½ orange peel, all must be brought to a boil. Add the juice of 2 lemons and the juice of one

orange to the mix, add one teaspoon of potato starch mixed into a paste and added to the boiling water. After this has cooled 2 egg yolks should be stirred in.

Apfelschalet for Pesach

8 egg yolks, ¼ lb sugar mixed well, ¼ lb almonds, 2 tablespoons matzo meal, some cinnamon, some grated lemon peel, and 8 peeled and chopped up apples added last and mixed well. The egg whites should be beaten to a foam.

Cookies (Crescent Cookies)

150 grams of butter, 70 grams of sugar, ¼ lb peeled almonds, 200 grams of meal, 2 packages of vanilla sugar. After the dough is made the cookies are shaped into little crescents and baked. Then the croissants are rolled in the powder and vanilla sugar (which was mixed before). You don't need to grease the pan where you bake the cookies.

III. Recipes from the family cookbook created by Deborah Roth-Howe.

Roth Birthday Cake (chocolate cake)

1 stick plus 1 Tbsp sweet butter

2 1/2 cups flour

1 cup sugar

3 tsp baking powder

5 eggs, separated

1/2 tsp baking soda

1/4 lb. Baker's German Sweet Chocolate, grated

3/4 cup strong coffee, cooled

1 heaping Tbsp Droste's cocoa

1/2 tsp cinnamon

1/4 tsp cloves

Cream butter with sugar. Add egg yolks, one at a time. In separate bowl, combine grated Baker's chocolate with cinnamon, cloves, flour, baking powder and baking soda. Gradually add flour mixture and coffee to butter mixture. Gently fold in beaten egg whites. Bake in greased springform pan at 350 for 40 minutes. When cooled, slice in half horizontally and cover bottom half with butter cream. Decorate top with more butter cream.

Butter Cream:

12 Tbsp sweet butter

3/4 cup sugar (extra fine sugar makes it less granular)

3 egg yolks

A few tsp of cold, strong coffee (to taste)

Mix sugar and butter well. Add egg yolks individually. Very slowly add cooled coffee until desired taste and consistency is obtained.

Grandma Toni's Kirschen Auflauf

6 Tbsp butter

1/2 cup sugar

3 eggs, separated

1 cup flour

1 tsp baking powder

2 cans sour cherries, drained and sprinkled with a little sugar 1 hour prior to baking

Mix butter and sugar. Add egg yolks, baking powder and flour. Beat egg whites until stiff and fold into batter. Pour into buttered baking pan and top with sour cherries (cherries will sink into the batter). Bake at 350 until browned.

Grandma Toni's Bienenstich

Dough:

4 cups flour

1/2 cup sugar

1 stick sweet butter, room temp

pinch of salt

2 pkg yeast,
   softened in 1/2 cup warm water

warm milk

Topping:

3/4 to 1 cup sugar

10 Tbsp sweet butter

2 Tbsp milk

1 pkg vanilla sugar

1 cup ground almonds

To make dough, let yeast proof in warm water. In separate bowl, mix flour, sugar, butter and salt. Add yeast and mix. Add warm milk until mixture is dough consistency. Knead the dough. Roll it out onto a greased cookie sheet. Spread the topping and let rise. To make topping, slowly melt butter over very low heat. Add sugar and stir. Add almonds and milk. Stir continuously until well-mixed, then remove from heat and let cool. When mixture is warm, spread it over the yeast dough. Let rise 1 hour. Bake at 325 for 20 minutes, or until bottom is brown.

Grandma Toni's Nut cake

Cake

9 eggs, separated

1 1/4 cup sugar

8 oz. ground almonds

Glaze

6 oz semisweet chocolate chips

small amount of water

1 Tbsp Crisco

juice and peel of 1 lemon   1 tsp rum extract
1/3 tsp baking powder

Mix egg yolks with sugar. Add remaining ingredients and mix well. Beat egg whites and fold them into batter. Place in an ungreased springform pan. Bake 45–60 minutes at 350. When cake is taken out of oven, immediately place pan upside down over waxed paper. Let cake cool in this position. When cool, separate cake from pan by running a sharp knife along sides and bottom. When completely cooled, cover with glaze which is made by melting chocolate in water and adding Crisco and rum extract.

Toni's brothers Hugo and Louis Stern,
Roth, Germany, c. 1935

Toni's mother Berta Stern, Roth, Germany

Walter with his grandfather Herz Stern, in Roth, Germany, c. 1934

Selma's father, Herz Stern, Roth, Germany, c. 1935

Markus (on right), with parents, grandmother, and
brothers in Nieder-Ohmen, Germany, c. 1912

Markus Roth as a young man, c. 1918, Germany

Selma Stern Roth and Markus Roth, c. 1925, Germany

Selma Stern Roth with her children Irene, Walter, and
Herbert, c. 1929, Roth, Germany

Left, Markus, in
Roth, Germany,
c. 1930

Below, Markus,
Helen, Toni,
Chicago, c. 1945

Ray School, Hyde Park, Chicago, 1943.
Walter is in the front row, 4th from right; and
Irene is in the second row, 4th from right.

Clockwise from left: Markus, Helen, Herb, Elsa Lazar
Roth, Walter, Irene, Toni, Chicago, c. 1949

Toni and Markus, Chicago, 1960

Markus,
Chicago, c. 1945

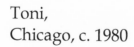

Toni,
Chicago, c. 1980

Backyard, 6840 S. Euclid in Jackson Park Highlands, Chicago, c. 1965. From left, Toni, Herb, Irene, Gitta Fajerstein, Walter, Helen, Markus, Sam Fajerstein

Markus, Helen, Toni, Chicago, 1960, at Helen's graduation from the College at the University of Chicago

Markus with grandson Ari Roth, South Shore, Chicago, c. 1963

Toni with grand-daughter Miriam Roth, Chicago, 1965

Toni with grandchildren Judy, Ari, and Miriam Roth,
Chicago, c. 1975

Toni with grandson Mark Dittmer, at Toni's 95th
birthday celebration, Chicago, 1993

Toni with granddaughter Debbie Roth-Howe and daughter-in-law Elsa Roth, at Toni's 95th birthday cele-bration, Chicago, 1993

Toni with her children and their spouses at her 95th birthday celebration, 1993. Clockwise from bottom left, Chaya, Walter, Lowell, Herb, Elsa, Toni, Helen

Toni with great-grandson Miko Zeldes-Roth, c. 1997

Toni with great-grandson Jonah Raider-Roth, 1994

Toni with great-granddaughter Emma Raider-Roth, 1997

Toni with great-granddaughters Isabel and Sophie Roth
and granddaughter-in-law Kate Schecter, c. 1995

Left, Emma, Jonah, and Talia Raider-Roth.

Below, Walter, Chaya Roth, grandchildren Miko and Tema Zeldes-Roth

This page and following: seven pages from Toni's
Chicago recipe book.

Apfelkuchen

1¼ cups flour 1 tablespoon Sugar a
little Salt ½ Teaspoon Baking powder 2
tablespoon Sweet cream ¼ lb. Butter.
Der Teich kommt in die Form. Die Äpfel
werden in dünne Scheiben darauf geschnitten
¼ cup Zucker und Zimmt wird durch
einander gemischt und dann über die Äpfel
gestreut. Man kann fein geschnittene Nüsse
darüber streuen. Zuletzt giesst man drei
Teelöffel Sweet cream über die Äpfel
Der Kuchen wird ungefähr 45 Minuten gebacken bei 325 to 350 Degree.

Matzemehl Torte, auch für Pessach

Man nimmt 8 Eier, 2 Tassen Zucker, 2 Tassen
Matzemehl, Saft von einer Zitrone und
von der Schale abgerieben zwei geriebene
Äpfel und etwas Baking powder. Das
Eiweiss wird zu Schnee geschlagen.

Nußtorte, auch für Pessach.

Man nimmt 9 Eggs, ½ lb Zucker ½ lb
gemahlene Nüsse, Saft von einer Lemon
und von der Schale abgerieben, etwas
baking powder. Eiweiss wird zu Schnee
geschlagen.

Bienenstich
man macht einen Teich und dann
dann präpariert man 190 gr. Butter

160 gr. Zucker 1 Päckchen Vanille zucker
100 gr. geriebene gemahlene Mandeln und
1 Eßlöffel milk. Die Butter läßt man
warm werden daß sie dünn wird dann
erst den zucker vanille sugar, die Mandeln
und zuletzt die milk. Alles läßt man
einige Minuten kochen. Den teich
welchen man schon vorher auf ein Kuchen
blech ausgewollt hat. Die gekockte masse
tut man dann auf den Kuchen daß
der Teich denn vollständig bedeckt ist
Der Kuchen wird ungefähr 20 Minuten
gebacken bei 350 degree. Ein Päckchen
Vanillezucker ist etwas weniger denn 2 Teelöffel

Rahm Torte

man macht einen gewöhnlichen mürben
Teich. Für oben drauf nimmt man
2 große Gläser saure cream 4 Eigelb
1 Päckchen Vanille sugar, die Schale von
einer Zitrone abgerieben, 1 Eßlöffel klein
zucker nach Geschmack. man kann auch
Raisins darunter tun. Das Eiweiß
wird zu Schnee geschlagen. Die masse
schüttet man dann auf den Kuchen
Ein Kuchen backt man bei 325 bis 350
degree bis er gut genug gebacken ist.

Marble Cake

3/4 cup butter, 2 cup sugar, 4 Eggs.
3/4 cup milk, 3 cup flour. 4 Teaspoon
Baking powder, 1/4 lb chocolate
(grinded), a little cinnamon a very

gebacken. Denn werden die [...]
in Puder und Vanille zucker [...]
varher gemengt hat) gewälzt [...]
bleibt wo man die Cookies [...]
will darf man nicht schmieren [...]

Zitronen Cream (Pudding)
6 Eggs 6 Table spoon Sugar werden [...]
bis dieses anfängt dick zu werden [...]
nimt man den Saft von 3 Zitronen
Wein und 1 Teaspoon Potato Starch
alles wird zum kochen gebracht [...]
es anfängt dick zu werden muß
sofort abgestellt werden, damit [...]
nicht anbrennt darf die Flamme [...]
hoch gestellt werden. Nachdem [...]
abgestellt ist muß nach einem [...]
gerührt werden, Wenn dieser [...]
ist kommt der Schnee darauf [...]

little cloves (otherwise it will get
the Toast too strong) 1/2 Teaspoon Vanille.
Die Butter rührt man erst dann den Zucker
Eggs dieses wird gut gerührt dann
kommt das ~~Salt~~ Mehl unter welches
Backingpowder gemischt ist und dann
die Milk.   man muß darauf achten daß
der Teig nicht zu dünn wird andernfalls
muß Iman weniger Milk nehmen.
man nimmt ein kleiner Teil von dem
Teich unter welchen man die chocolade
und das gewürz mischt und tut dieses
lagenweise in die Form. Den Kuchen
backt man bei ungefähr 350 degree ver-
ungefähr 50 Minuten!

Chocolate Torte

1/4 lb. Butter gut verrührt dann 300 gr
Sugar ebenfalls gut rühren dann so
~~300 gr Flour 1/2 Glas Coffee~~ nimmt
man 4 Eigelb wenn dieses alles gut
gerührt ist dann nimmt man 300 gr
Flour 1/2 Glas Coffee einen Eßlöffel
oder etwas mehr Kakao, 1/4 lb geriebene
chocolade ein päckchen Backing powder
etwas cinnemon sehr wenig cloves und
etwas Zitron. Wenn dieses alles gut
gerührt ist, tut man das Eiweiß welches zu
Schnee geschlagen ist, darunter. Der
Kuchen wird ungefähr 50 Min gebacken
dann muß man probieren ob es lange
genug ist u der Kuchen gar ist.

Zitronen Suppe

8 gläser Water 1 glas Zucker 1/2 Zitronen
Schale , 1/2 Ap Orange schale wird zum
Kochen gebracht . Den Saft 2 Lemon
und den Saft von einer Orange darin
tut man ein Teaspoon Potato starch
anrühren und schüttet dieses in das
Kochende Wasser. Nachdem dieses eb.
gekühlt ist werden zwei Eigelb ein=
gerührt

Chocolate Pudding, kalt gerührt

man nimmt 250 gr. Chocolate 1 Wein
glas Wein 1 Päckchen Vanille sugar
7 Eigelb das Eiweiß wird zu Schnee
geschlagen. Die Chocolate läst man
auf niedrigem Feuer dünn werden
bevor man diese auf die Flamme stellt
commt der Wein darunter und Vanille
sugar man muß rühren damit es
nicht im Pot anhängt . man stellt
es vom Herd und tut ein Eigelb
nach dem anderen darunter wo man
auch dabei rühren muß. Zuletzt
kommt der Schnee darunter

Cookies Hörnchen

150 gr. Butter, 70 gr. Zucker, 1/4 lb geschälte
Almon ≈ 200 gr. Mehl, 1 Päckchen Vanille
Zucker (das sind ungefähr 2 Teaspoon)
Nachdem der Teig gemacht ist werden
die Cookies zu Hörnchen geformt und

Käse Kuchen.

Für einen Kuchen rechnet man 2 1/2 lb.
Matte 3 Eggs etwas Salt, Sugar nach
Geschmack, 1 grosses Glas Sauer cream
Vanille sugar und Rosinen und etwas
Flour.

Sträussel Kuchen (Hefe teich

Dazu rechnet man auf 6 lb. Mehl 1 lb.
Butter 1 lb. Zucker etwas Salt (Hefe)
Feast und Milk.
Für die Sträussel nimmt man
4 Table spoon Flour 3 Table spoon Sugar
1 Päckchen Vanille etwas Zimmt 1/4 lb. Butter
die Butter last man dünn werden.

Kreppel

Zwei lb Flour dazu rechnet man
3/4 lb Zucker, 3/4 lb Butter, 5 Eggs
für 7 ct cent feast.

Kirschen auflauf

man nimmt 75 gr. Butter, 1/4 lb.
Zucker 3 Eigelb, 1/4 lb Flour 1 Päckchen
Backing Powder. Erst rührt man
Eigelb mit Zucker dann kommt alles
andere dazu und wenn alles gerührt
ist dann kommt Der Schnee darunter.
den Teich schüttet man in die Form
Die entkernte Sauer Kirschen welche

man 1 Stunde vorher gezuckert hatte
läst man durch einen Sträuner ab-
laufen. und tut sie nachher auf den
Kuchen & läst dieses backen.

Apfelschalet for Pessach

8 Eigelb 1/4 lb Zucker wird gut ver-
spührt 1/4 lb Mandeln, 2 Esslöffel
Matzenmehl etwas Zitrone abgerieben
= 8 Äpfel werden gerieben welche zuletzt darunter gerührt werden. Das
Eiweiß wird zu Schnee geschlagen

Butter cookies

1 lb Sweet butter 2 egg yolk, 1 cup
sugar 3 1/2 cup Flour 1 Teaspoon
vanilla. Everything will be mixed
together when the doe is allright
put it in the Ice box for 1 hour
untll the doug ist hart. Then you
can macke the cookies and bake
it right away.

Cookies

1 small Package cream cheese 1 Stick
Butter 1 cup flour, salt. When you
macke de cookies Put jelly between
in the cookies and bake it.

I dont know if Backing powder has to be

EPILOGUE

Recently I woke up with a memory or dream of being a little boy tossing in bed between my mother (Selma) and my father. I recognized the bed as being upstairs in our old house in Roth where my mother and father slept. I seemed be to playing with them, and then I woke up. It left me with a happy feeling and it quickly reminded me of an event that I remember from shortly after Selma died. I remember waking up and running to the window, where I saw an angel. It was the size of an eagle, and with powerful wings. It hovered by the window and then disappeared. After that I would often go to the window to look for it but it never reappeared. I recall that when I when I would sit with my grandfather Herz on the Lahn River and ask him where my mother was, he would point to the sky and say "look for the clouds, for she is in heaven."

Made in the USA
Middletown, DE
12 November 2014